AF836110

AFRICAN POLITICAL, ECONOMIC, AND SECURITY ISSUES

TUNISIA

SOCIAL, ECONOMIC AND ENVIRONMENTAL ISSUES

AFRICAN POLITICAL, ECONOMIC, AND SECURITY ISSUES

Additional books in this series can be found on Nova's website under the Series tab.

Additional e-books in this series can be found on Nova's website under the eBook tab.

AFRICAN POLITICAL, ECONOMIC, AND SECURITY ISSUES

TUNISIA

SOCIAL, ECONOMIC AND ENVIRONMENTAL ISSUES

EUNICE WAGNER
EDITOR

nova publishers
New York

Copyright © 2016 by Nova Science Publishers, Inc.

All rights reserved. No part of this book may be reproduced, stored in a retrieval system or transmitted in any form or by any means: electronic, electrostatic, magnetic, tape, mechanical photocopying, recording or otherwise without the written permission of the Publisher.

We have partnered with Copyright Clearance Center to make it easy for you to obtain permissions to reuse content from this publication. Simply navigate to this publication's page on Nova's website and locate the "Get Permission" button below the title description. This button is linked directly to the title's permission page on copyright.com. Alternatively, you can visit copyright.com and search by title, ISBN, or ISSN.

For further questions about using the service on copyright.com, please contact:
Copyright Clearance Center
Phone: +1-(978) 750-8400 Fax: +1-(978) 750-4470 E-mail: info@copyright.com.

NOTICE TO THE READER

The Publisher has taken reasonable care in the preparation of this book, but makes no expressed or implied warranty of any kind and assumes no responsibility for any errors or omissions. No liability is assumed for incidental or consequential damages in connection with or arising out of information contained in this book. The Publisher shall not be liable for any special, consequential, or exemplary damages resulting, in whole or in part, from the readers' use of, or reliance upon, this material. Any parts of this book based on government reports are so indicated and copyright is claimed for those parts to the extent applicable to compilations of such works.

Independent verification should be sought for any data, advice or recommendations contained in this book. In addition, no responsibility is assumed by the publisher for any injury and/or damage to persons or property arising from any methods, products, instructions, ideas or otherwise contained in this publication.

This publication is designed to provide accurate and authoritative information with regard to the subject matter covered herein. It is sold with the clear understanding that the Publisher is not engaged in rendering legal or any other professional services. If legal or any other expert assistance is required, the services of a competent person should be sought. FROM A DECLARATION OF PARTICIPANTS JOINTLY ADOPTED BY A COMMITTEE OF THE AMERICAN BAR ASSOCIATION AND A COMMITTEE OF PUBLISHERS.

Additional color graphics may be available in the e-book version of this book.

Library of Congress Cataloging-in-Publication Data

Names: Wagner, Eunice, editor.
Title: Tunisia : social, economic and environmental issues / editors: Eunice Wagner.
Other titles: African political, economic, and security issues series.
Description: Hauppauge, New York : Nova Science Publishers, Inc., 2016. | Series: African political, economic, and security issues | Includes index.
Identifiers: LCCN 2016037378 | ISBN 9781536100617 (Hardcover)
Subjects: LCSH: Tunisia--Economic conditions. | Tunisia--Social conditions. | Tunisia--Environmental conditions. | Sustainable development--Tunisia.
Classification: LCC HC820 .T864 2016 | DDC 330.9611--dc23 LC record available at https://lccn.loc.gov/2016037378

Published by Nova Science Publishers, Inc. † New York

CONTENTS

PREFACE

Tunisia is located in North Africa, on the border of the Mediterranean. Covering 162,155 km, it is characterized by a temperate climate in the north, with mild rainy winters and hot summers, and a desert type of climate in the south. Tunisia is an arid country on the major part of its territory. This book reviews the social, economic and environmental issues of Tunisia. Chapter One discusses irrigation and soil salinity of the country. Chapter Two assesses the effects of deficit irrigation on gross margin and water use efficiency of potato crops, irrigated with subsurface drip irrigation, in a semiarid area of central Tunisia. Chapter Three provides a performance evaluation of AquaCrop in simulating soil water content, canopy cover, and root development for maize conducted under subsurface drip irrigation. Chapter Four presents new angles on analyzing Domestic Solar Water Heating systems (DSWHs) deployment in Tunisia by analyzing both the energetic and the economic potential through a case study. Chapter Five studies the potential offered by the use of a PV/T solar collector in Tunisian households to supply electricity and domestic hot water simultaneously. Chapter Six contributes to the understanding of the epidemiology of enteric viruses in Tunisia and underlines the need of an environmental surveillance program and official viral controls for treated wastewater. Chapter Seven focuses on the climate change effects of evapotranspiration estimated by different empirical models under the Mediterranean environment.

Chapter 1 - Location of Tunisia between the Mediterranean and the Sahara, is an arid country on the major part of its territory. This aridity combined with variability Mediterranean climate makes water a resource both scarce and unevenly distributed in time and space. Tunisia is ranked by international organizations (World Bank, FAO, UNESCO) as being among the least endowed with groundwater resources countries in the Mediterranean basin.

Salinity is a major environmental factor limiting plant growth and productivity. In arid and semi-arid regions of the world salinization is exacerbated by the development of soil sodicity, especially those regions with limited rainfall, high evapotranspiration, and high temperature. Sodicity is associated with the use of irrigation water containing high concentrations of sodium. Soil and water salinity in the arid regions are continuously increasing. The present contribution concerns the state of water resources in Tunisia, their management and the necessary services for an efficient water use. The physical major constraints are specified, for better irrigation practices in the field, water management modes, in particular with regards to water users associations

Chapter 2 - In Tunisia, the expansion of irrigated area and the semiarid climate make it compulsory to adopt strategies of water management to increase water use efficiency. Subsurface drip irrigation (SDI), providing the application of high frequency small irrigation volumes below the soil surface have been increasingly used to enhance irrigation efficiency. Deficit irrigation has shown successful results with a large number of crops in various countries.

Objective of this paper was to assess the effects of deficit irrigation on gross margin and water use efficiency of potatoes crop, irrigated with subsurface drip irrigation, in a semiarid area of central Tunisia. After assessing the validity of FAO-56 spreadsheet program to well simulate soil water status in the root zone, water use efficiency (WUE) was evaluated based on crop yield and simulated actual evapotranspiration. At the same time, irrigation water use efficiency (IWUE) was determined as the ration between crop yield and the amount of water supply to the crop (irrigation).

Field experiments, were carried out in Central Tunisia (10 ◦ 33’ 47.0” E, 35 ◦ 58’ 8.1 ◦ N, 19 m a.s.l) on a potatoes crop planted in a sandy loam soil, during the growing season 2014, from 15 January to 6 May. Soil water status was monitored in two plots (T1 and T2) maintained under the same management, except for irrigation volumes, provided by a SDI system. More particular, irrigation was scheduled according to the average water content measured in the root zone, with a total of 8 watering, with timing ranging between one and three hours in T1, and between about half-an-hour and one-hour and a-half, in T2. FAO-56 was validated according the average soil water content in all tubes and all observation depths with RMSE values, equal to 0.012 cm^3cm^{-3} and 0.028 cm^3cm^{-3}, respectively for T1 and T2. Simulated actual evapotranspiration in T1 was equal to the potential evapotranspiration.

However, it resulted lower than potential evapotranspiration. WUE resulted equal to 32 Kg/m^3 and 16 Kg/m^3, whereas IWUE was equal to 31.7 Kg/m^3 and 45.70 Kg/m^3 for treatments T1 and T2. In terms of gross margin, T1 were more efficient than T2. This finding is directly related to sheep price of water, although its scarcity.

The experimental results and model simulations provided useful guidelines for a more sustainable use of irrigation water.

Chapter 3 - In this study, AquaCrop model was evaluated for maize (*Zea mays* L.) in the experimental site of Chott Mariem, Sousse (semi-arid climate), with data from two companions corn grown in the years 2008 and 2010. The crop was led under subsurface drip irrigation (SDI) to 20 cm deep. The simulation was repeatedly made on three parameters to know soil water content (SWC), canopy cover and root development. The best wedging SWC belonged to statistical estimators values ranging from 1.1 to 3.34 for the RMSE, between [0-1] for R^2 and efficiency EF (often positive) values very close to zero for the CRM (-0.001 for the water content to 20 cm depth), and a $\approx$ 1 CD. Concerning the canopy cover calibration, the wedging settled with R^2 in the range of 0.92 seen fit enough (the ideal is $R^2 = 1$), and root development was rigged with a RMSE in the range of 3.13, an $R^2 = 0.92$, a CRM, CD and EF in the desired standards. Although the quality of the calibration for all three parameters was considered good enough through graphics and estimators calculated, validation, concerning only the water content and root development, gave a perfect complement to only the root growth ($R^2 = 0.99$). The validation of the moisture content with data of the partner 2008, indeed gave negative values of the efficiency EF in the majority of the depths, so showing that the experimental values are better than those feigned. This regression of the quality of validation was, according to us, the result of the various defects of the model to know the not consideration of the depth of the subsurface drip irrigation system, the conservatives parameters are not precise for a specific range and the fixation of the own percentages in sand, silt and clay by the user, is not possible.

Chapter 4 - This paper presents new angles on analyzing Domestic Solar Water Heating systems (DSWHs) deployment in Tunisia by analyzing both the energetic and the economic potential through a case study related to Tunisian scenario. In this scenario the authors evaluate the performance and the life cycle perspective of the two most popular DSWHs over the recent years (i.e., DSWH with flat-plate solar collector, installation No. 1, and DSWHs with evacuated-tube solar collector, installation No. 2). The dynamic behavior of DSWHs according to Tunisian data weather is achieved by means of TRNSYS simulation. Results show that the installations No. 1 and No. 2 supplies 1555.38 kWh/year and 1618.75 kWh/ year of energy. Using estimates from the demand-side of hot water for a typical Tunisian household composed of 4-5 persons, the paper evaluates the economic potential of DSWHs in saving electricity and reducing carbon dioxide emissions. Results show that the annual savings in electrical energy and payback period relatively to the No. 1, were 1316 kWh/year and 8 years based on electric water heater, or 306 m3 gas saving and 6 years payback period based on gas water heater, respectively. For the installation No. 2 the annual electricity saving and payback period were 1459 kWh/year and 10 years based on electric water heater, or 410 m3gas saving and 7.5 years payback period based on gas water heater, respectively. The life cycle savings by installing the solar system instead of buying electricity/gas/town gas to satisfy hot water needs is about 3969 $ (Installation No. 1) and 4400.34 $ (Installation No. 2) for electricity backup and is about 1517.76 $ (Installation No. 1) and 2035.24 $ (Installation No. 2) for gas/town gas backup. From an environmental point of view the annual GHG emission per house is reduced by 27800 tCO2.

Chapter 5 - The endeavor of this chapter is to study the potential offered by the expenditure of a PV/T solar system in Tunisian households. This investigation is performed according to two-folded approaches. Firstly, outdoor experiments were carried out during July 2014 for both passive and active mode. An exhaustive energy and exergy analysis was then performed to evaluate the instantaneous thermal and the electrical exergy outputs of the PV/T system. The results showed that the maximum instantaneous thermal and electric energy efficiency in active mode are about 50 and 15%, respectively. It was found also that the maximum thermal and electric exergy efficiencies were about 50 and 14.8%, respectively. The second approach is the evaluation of the monthly/annual performances of the PV/T solar system under typical climate area of Tunisia by using TRNSYS program. The results showed that the active mode enhances the electric efficiency and the exergy of the PV/T solar system by 3 and 2.5% points, respectively. The results showed that the optimized PV/T solar system covert the major part of the hot water and the electric needs of Tunisian household's with an expected annual average gain of about 14.60 and 5.33%, respectively. An economic appraisal was performed.

Chapter 6 - The reuse of treated wastewater in irrigation and to refill the aquifer became a common strategy in Tunisia to palliate the lack of water resources. However, sewage treatment processes currently used are only partially effective to remove viruses and consequently discharge of contaminated treated wastewater is a potential source of viral infections. Hepatitis A virus (HAV), hepatitis E virus (HEV), norovirus (NoV), rotavirus (RV), enterovirus (EV), astrovirus (AsV), sapovirus (SaV), adenovirus (AdV) and aichi virus (AiV) are, among enteric viruses, the major waterborne pathogens, predominantly transmitted via the faecal-oral route, and important agents implicated in gastroenteritis or hepatitis outbreaks. They are released in large quantities in raw wastewater and can survive for long periods in several environments which present an important public health hazards. Due to their persistence and low infectious dose, enteric viruses can easily infect people via water or food. Although Tunisia is considered as an endemic country for enteric viruses, routine surveillance of viral wastewater quality is not performed and data on viral epidemiology are limited. In this review the authors provide an overview on the prevalence of the most common enteric viruses in wastewater from different regions of Tunisia including socioeconomic data and seasonal distribution when available. Indeed, efficiency of different wastewater treatment processes for viral reduction is discussed in order to evaluate the risk associated to the wastewater in the country. Data show that RV, HAV, EV and NoV are constantly present in both raw and treated wastewater with high prevalence. Differences in the incidence of these viruses in wastewater within the country are linked to variations in socioeconomic and sanitary conditions, geographic area and climate. The authors describe also the genetic diversity of multiple pathogenic enteric viruses in sewage. Different viral reduction rates are observed demonstrating the difficulty of the present biological treatments to provide virus-free wastewater effluents. This review contributes to the understanding of the epidemiology of enteric viruses in Tunisia and underlines the need of an environmental surveillance program and official viral controls for treated wastewater. Therefore, efforts should focus on the enhancing of sewage treatment technologies to avoid a social and public health hazard.

Chapter 7 - Water scarcity is among the main problems to be faced by many societies on the World in the XXIst century. It is due the combination between the increase of urban and industrial needs and the effects of climate change. The approach to estimate climate change impacts on water resources consist on union between climate model outputs and hydrological models. However, due to the coarse resolution of Global Circulation Models (GCM), their outputs should been downscaled to match the scale of interest for an impact study. In literature, two downscaling methods have been showed. The first approach is Dynamical Downscaling (DD) and the second is Statistical Downscaling (SD) approach. Until now, the impacts of climate change on evapotranspiration have not been conclusively determined. Generally decrease in rainfall and increase in temperature will result in increase in evapotranspiration. In this context, the sustainable management of water resources requires a good control of the hydrological terms. Evapotranspiration, as the major component of water cycle, is the main way for water consumption of earth system. The accurate estimation of evapotranspiration has a great importance in hydrological modeling, irrigation planning and water resources management. In the Mediterranean regions, especially in Tunisia, the main climate is characterized by an important evaporation potential. This particularity is due to the conjugation between different climatic parameters. In Tunisia, irrigated agriculture uses about 83% of the total water resources. Thus, estimating evapotranspiration is the most important step for calculating crop water requirements that has a special economic importance in rationalization of water consumption in the agricultural field. Physically-based and empirical methods to estimate evapotranspiration are evaluated in different climatic environment under current climate conditions but also under recent, and in a changing climate.

In: Tunisia
Editor: Eunice Wagner

ISBN: 978-1-53610-061-7
© 2016 Nova Science Publishers, Inc.

Chapter 1

IRRIGATION AND SOIL SALINITY IN TUNISIA

Amel Belhaj Mguidiche*[1]*, Boutheina Douh*[1,2]*,
***Hiba Ghazouani*[2] *and Abdelhamid Boujelben* [2]**
[1]Regional Field Crops Research Center (CRRGC) Béja-Tunisia
[2]Higher Institute of Agronomy of Chott Mariem Sousse Tunisia

ABSTRACT

Location of Tunisia between the Mediterranean and the Sahara, is an arid country on the major part of its territory. This aridity combined with variability Mediterranean climate makes water a resource both scarce and unevenly distributed in time and space. Tunisia is ranked by international organizations (World Bank, FAO, UNESCO) as being among the least endowed with groundwater resources countries in the Mediterranean basin.

Salinity is a major environmental factor limiting plant growth and productivity. In arid and semi-arid regions of the world salinization is exacerbated by the development of soil sodicity, especially those regions with limited rainfall, high evapotranspiration, and high temperature. Sodicity is associated with the use of irrigation water containing high concentrations of sodium. Soil and water salinity in the arid regions are continuously increasing. The present contribution concerns the state of water resources in Tunisia, their management and the necessary services for an efficient water use. The physical major constraints are specified, for better irrigation practices in the field, water management modes, in particular with regards to water users associations

Keywords: Tunisa, irrigation, salinity

Introduction

Tunisia is located in North Africa, on the border of the Mediterranean. Covering 162,155 km^2, it is characterized by a temperate climate in the north, with mild rainy winters and hot summers, and a desert type of climate in the south, Tunisia is an arid country on the major part of its territory. It is the least country endowed in underground water resources in the Mediterranean basin. The volume of water available (surface and groundwater) per year per capita is estimated at 450 m^3. This ratio will be 315 m^3/person/year in 2030 when the population will reach 13 million inhabitants (NSI, 1996).

The average annual rainfall in Tunisia was less than 100 mm in south to over 1200 mm in northwest Ratio between maximum and minimum rainfall change from 4.4 to 15.8 from the North to the South, representing the temporal irregularity and variability from one region to another (DG/RE, 2003).

Water Resource in Tunisia

Conventional water resources in Tunisia were 4670 million m^3/year, in which 2.7 million m^3/year on average in surface water and 1.97 million m^3/year underground water. Unconventional potential resource, limited in treated domestic wastewater was 250 million m^3. The quality of surface water, evaluated by its degree of salinity, change according the origin of the resource. Considering that salinity less than 1.5g/l is acceptable, then approximately 72% of the surface resources may be considered had a good quality. Water quality also change across the country with 82% of the water resources in the north considered good quality, 48% of that in the center and only 3% in the south.

Like surface water, groundwater is characterized by unequal allocation and variable quality in terms of salinity. Groundwater is distributed as follows:

- The north has 55% of the shallow groundwater resources and only 18% of the deep groundwater resources;
- The center provides 30% of the shallow resources and 24% of the deep resources;

- The south provides 15% of the shallow resources and has 58% of the deep resources.

Good quality groundwater is found in only 8% of shallow water and 20% of deep aquifers. If one accepts that saline water up to 3g/l can be used in the agricultural sector and for the production of drinking water, then approximately 36% of groundwater resources are not suited for these two sectors which are in increasing demand.

Another phenomenon, which affects quality of water, is drought. In drought period, salinity of water stored in shallow aquifers can reach 3.5 g/l due to over draft as resources are drawn down for both drinking and irrigation.

WATER IRRIGATION DEMAND

Irrigation in Tunisia currently consumes almost 83% of the volumes distributed to all sectors. Irrigated area was approximately 400 000 ha in 2010. Water consumption for the irrigation sector during the same period was 2.14 million m^3, ground water levels irrigated over 150, 000 hectares, while the deep levels irrigated over 70,000 hectares, for a total of 220,000 hectares. Dams irrigated 130,000 hectares. Treated wastewater served to irrigate 7,000 hectares, and the rest is irrigated partly from pumping directly from temporary water sources and partly from natural sources.

Table 1. Spatial Distribution of Water Resources in Tunisia [million cubic meters]

	Far North	North	Center	South	Country total
Regional surface (%)	3			62	100%
Supply of surface water (millions m^3)	960	1230	320	190	2700
Groundwater (millions m^3)	395		216	108	719
Deep groundwater (millions of m^3)	269		326	822	1417
Total potential resource (millions of m^3)	2854		862	1120	4836
%	59		18	23	100

Table 2. Breakdown of Salinity of Water Resources (%)

	Salinity < 1.5	1.5 < salinity < 3	Salinity > 3	Total
Surface water	72	22	6	100
Groundwater	8	32	60	100
Deep groundwater	20	57	23	100
Total	47	34	19	100

In 2003, 260,000 hectares (70% of the total irrigated land) was equipped with water conservation systems including drip irrigation, sprinklers, pipes and watertight channels. A group of collectives (AICs) manage 135,000 hectares of irrigated lands. These associations are responsible for the maintenance of the irrigation network and the distribution of water to their members. Drinking water in metropolitan areas is managed by a national company that distributes 350 million m^3 per year to meet the needs of 1.5 million subscribers. The volume is expected to increase to 450 million m^3 by 2030. In rural areas, the administration of the drinking water distribution system is handled by cooperative associations (AIC).

MAJOR PHYSICAL CONSTRAINTS IN THE PRACTICE OF IRRIGATION

Tunisia will face a demand for more and more important, than the volume of all conventional water resources regularized. For surface resource particularly the silting dams currently one of the problems thorniest, which reduces the volume of stored water. The water shortage if it occurs is damped by mobilizing new resources in unconventional water, mainly from treated wastewater and brackish water.

Drought

A hydrological drought year is defined by 40% compared to the rainfall contribution means: In case of widespread drought, supply of low water was 150Mm^3 (DG/ETH, 1998).

The drought management should not be limited to actions at the time of drought but should rather prepare for drought and manage in order to ensure the revival of post drought campaign.

Salinity of Irrigation Water

Use of saline water was a problem that has attracted of researchers in Tunisia for over 60 years. CRUESI experiments (1970) represent a Tunisian reference for using salt water in irrigation without major risks, respecting certain rules of water management and soil. The fact remains that these rules are not always respected by farmers.

Given the scarcity of water and its poor quality, the problems related to salinization and water loggings are quite common, especially in irrigated areas of the Valley Mejerda and oasis.

In Tunisia, the total amount of moving salts in the landscape constantly increases over time. In irrigated areas, the objective was to remove salts without affecting downstream areas where the groundwater underlying (Ennabli, 1995).

At the scale of the plot and in the case of deficient drainage, capillary action in the water relations of crop is a major salinization process in Tunisia. Increasing severity of problems related to use salt water to the plot and to drainage excess incentive to study the evolution land irrigated water with salt water. Evaluation of performance of drainage systems and the determination of water and salt balance, the rehabilitation of saline soils by drainage and irrigation integrating leaching requirements; conditions of using of salt water over 4 g/l depending on the soil type.

SOIL SALINITY

Soil and water salinity in the arid regions are continuously increasing (Rus et al., 2002). Globally, more than 770,000 km^2 of the lands are affected by secondary salinization, 20% of the irrigated areas and about 2% of the agricultural lands (FAO, 2000). In Tunisia, soils affected by salts cover about 1.5 million hectares, around 10% of the total country area. About 30% of irrigated areas are affected by salts in different degrees (Hachicha, 2007).

They are found in the whole country but especially in the center and south that the aridity of the climate because their extension. (Hachicha et al., 1994).

Several geological formations are sources of soluble salts. Water runoff and drainage, enriched with soluble elements, flow to the lower parts of watersheds. From there, two cases will be presented the watershed has an outlet and salts then migrate down - this is the case of the Mejerda valley; where the catchment is endorheic and sebkha forms in the lower part. These phenomena occur throughout the year in the arid part of Tunisia and during the dry season in the Mediterranean part. They are either natural or caused by irrigation. Geochemically, solutions (surface water, groundwater or soil) evolve during their concentration, according to the neutral saline way (Gallali, 1980), which means that we observe, with increasing the concentration factor, the precipitation of certain salts in a specific order (calcite, gypsum, etc.) with the NaCl. There are also much less soluble compounds such as calcium carbonate and gypsum, or much more soluble as the bloedite and thenardite. These salts, chlorides, sulfates or carbonates, basic or compound, are distinguied by their solubility. In a homogeneous climatic region and for the same soil water regime, more salt is soluble; it will be more quickly and easily leached out of the profile and out of the watershed that gave it birth.

The spatial variability of soil salinity over the landscape is highly sensitive and controlled by a variety factors. These factors include soil factors (parent material, permeability, water table depth, groundwater quality and topography), management factors (irrigation and drainage) and climatic factors (rainfall and humidity) (Douaik et al., 2008). The characterization of soil salinity is generally done measuring the electric conductivity (EC) in a saturated soil paste or in aqueous extracts with different soil/water ratios and using a spectrometer (Ben Dor et al., 2008, Goldshleger et al., 2013). To elaborate detailed maps, density of soil samples using the previous technique is required, through an extensive design, which makes mapping time consuming and expensive.

Soil salinity occurs naturally in sea salt marshes or areas in which salt is already a part of the soil composition. This is called primary salinization, and any plants that grow here are adapted to the soil composition. Secondary salinization occurs when soils that once had a low concentration of salt become saltier because of irrigation and poor drainage (Zhu, 2007). The plants that grow on these soils are not adapted to tolerate salty conditions, thus, when soils become more saline, they struggle to thrive. Salts can also result in the deterioration of soil structure and a decreased capacity to hold water or aerate. Ideally, farmers should use fresh water to irrigate fields in arid regions, but because of the demand for fresh water in many other sectors, growers use water with a higher salt content such as ground water, drainage water, or treated wastewater (Yadav et al., 2011). The cations and anions correlated with salinity are Na^+, Ca^{2+}, Mg^{2+}, Cl^-, SO_4^{2-}, and HCO_3^- (Yadav et al., 2011). Excessive sodium and chloride ions are toxic to plants.

PLANT AND SALINITY

Salinity is a major abiotic factor limiting plant growth and fruit yield (Parada et al., 2006). It induces osmotic and toxic effects leading physiological, morphological and biochemical modifications; it causes growth inhibition, crop yield reduction, lower photosynthesis and respiration, nutritional deficiencies and inhibition of protein synthesis (Ashraf and Foolad, 2007). These phenomena have been observed in agricultural and horticultural crops, including tomato (Juan et al., 2005).

Salt has two major effects on plants: osmotic stress and ionic toxicity, both of which affect all major plant processes (Yadav et al., 2011). Plants are able to take up water and essential minerals because they have a higher water pressure than the soil under normal conditions. When salt stress occurs, the osmotic pressure of the soil solution is greater than that in plant cells. Thus, the plant cannot get enough water (Kader, 2010). In addition, its cells will have decreased turgor and its stomat will close to conserve water. Stomat closing can lead to less carbon fixation and the production of Reactive Oxygen Species (ROS) such as superoxide and singlet oxygen. ROS disrupts cell processes through damage to lipids, proteins, and nucleic acids (Parada and Das, 2005). Ionic toxicity occurs when concentrations of salts are imbalanced inside cells and inhibit cellular metabolism and processes. Sodium ions at the root surface disrupt plant nutrition of the similar cation potassium by inhibiting both potassium uptake and enzymatic activities within the cell. Potassium is an important nutrient in a plant, regulating over 50 enzymes (Kader, 2010). Essential for maintaining cell turgor pressure, creating membrane potential, and regulating enzymatic activities, potassium must be maintained at 100-200mM in the cytosol. Sodium, on the other hand, causes stress at concentrations higher than 10mM in the cytosol (Kader, 2010). Na^+ is a cation similar to K^+ and easily crosses the cell membrane. It also acts as an inhibitor to many enzymes, affecting metabolic processes. Calcium cations, however, protect some plants through signaling pathways that regulate potassium sodium transporters (Parida and Das, 2005). When a plant senses salt stress through transmembrane proteins or enzymes in the cytosol, the amount of calcium in the cytosol increases (Kader, 2010). Calcium is a second messenger important to many biochemical pathways and can aid plants in responding to salt stress. The osmotic and ionic stress induced by salinity can halt plant growth as the plant focuses its energy on conserving water and improving ionic balance. In order for plants to return to normal functioning and photosynthesis, the plant must facilitate its own detoxification damage must be prevented or lessened, homeostasis must be reestablished, and growth must resume (Zhu, 2001).

CONCLUSION

Tunisia will shortly be confronted with the problem of a water deficit between its consumptive uses and its water productivity. Conscious of this problem, managers and policy makers are giving particular attention to improvements in water supply and mobilization programs, to enhancements in water productivity with an integrated management perspective, to promotion of treated sewage water and its development, and to controlling the different economic sectors of water demand and protecting the available resources from losses and pollution.

REFERENCES

Ashraf, M., Foolad, M. R. Roles of glycine betaine and proline in improving. *Environ. Exp. Bot.* 59, 2007. 206-216.

Ben-Dor, E.; Goldshleger, N.; EshelMor, V. *Combined Active and Passive Remote Sensing Methods for Assessing Soil Salinity: A Case Study from Jezre'el Valley, Northern Israel.* In Remote Sensing of Soil Salinization: Impact on Land Management; Metternicht, G., Zinck, J. A., Eds.; CRC Press: Boca Raton, FL, USA, 2008; pp. 236-253.

DG/ETH. *Stratégie du secteur de líeau en Tunisie long terme 2030*: EAU 21 Rapport final, DG/ETH, Mars 1998.

Douaik, A.; Meirvenne, M.; Toth, T. *Stochastic Approaches for Space-Time Modeling and Interpolation of Soil Salinity.* In Remote Sensing of Soil Salinization: Impact on Land Management; Metternicht, G., Zinck, J. A., Eds.; CRC Press: Boca Raton, FL, USA, 2008; pp. 273-289.

FAO. *Global network on integrated soil management for sustainable use of salt effected soils.* 2000.

Gallali T. *Transferts sels-matière organique en zones arides méditerranéennes. Contribution à l'étudepédobiologique des sols salsodiques formés sur matériaux sédimentaires.* Thèse, doctoratd'État, université de Nancy I, 1980.

Goldshleger, N.; Chudnovsky, A.; Ben-Binyamin, R. Predicting salinity in tomato using soil reflectance spectra. *Int. J. Remote Sens.*, 34, 2013, 6079-6093.

Hachicha M, Job JO, Mtimet A. Les sols salés et la salinisation des sols en Tunisie. Sols de Tunisie, *Bulletin de la Direction des Sols*; (15) 1994: 270-341.

Hachicha, M. Les sols salés et leur mise en valeur en Tunisie. *Séch.* 18, 2007 45-50.

INS, *Statistiques de la Tunisie 1996.*

Jordán, M.; Navarro-Pedreño, J.; García-Sánchez, E.; Mateu, J.; Juan, P. Spatial dynamics of soil salinity under arid and semi-arid conditions: Geological and environmental implications. *Environ. Geol.*, 45, 2004. pp. 448-456.

Juan, M., Rosa, M., Rivero, M. R., Romero, L., Ruiz, J. M. Evaluation of some nutritional and biochemical indicators in selecting salt-resistant tomato cultivars. *Environ. Exp. Bot.* 54, 2005, pp. 193-201

Kader MAL, S. Cytosolic calcium and pH signaling in plants under salinity stress. *Plant Signal Behav.* 5(3): 2010, pp. 233-238.

Lebdi F. *Appui pour l'irrigation et la gestion des systemeshydrauliques.* In: Lamaddalena N. (ed.), Lebdi F. (ed.), Todorovic M. (ed.), Bogliotti C. (ed.). Irrigation systems performance. Bari: CIHEAM, 2005. pp. 193-203.

Parada, A. K., Das, A. B. Salt tolerance and salinity effects on plants, a review. *Ecot. Environ. Safety* 60, 2006, pp. 324-349.

Parada AK, Das AB 2005. Salt tolerance and salinity effects on plants: a review. *Ecotox. Environ. Safe.* 60:2005, pp. 324-349.

Rus, A. M., RioRíos, S., Olmos, E., Santa-Cruz, A., Bolarin, M. C. Long term culture modifies the salt responses of callus lines of salttolerant and salt-sensitive tomato species. *Plant Physiol.* 157, 2002. 413-420.

Tanji, K. *Salinity in the Soil Environment.* In Salinity: Environment-Plants-Molecules; Lauchli, A., Luttge., U., Eds.; Kluwer Academic Publisher: Dordrecht, The Netherlands, 2004; pp. 21-51.

Yadav S, Irfan M, Ahmad A, Hayat S Causes of salinity and plant manifestations to salt stress: A review. *J Environ Biol* 32: 2011. 667-685.

Yadav S, Irfan M, Ahmad A, Hayat S. Causes of salinity and plant manifestations to salt stress: A review. *J Environ Biol* 32: 2011 667-685.

Zhu JK. Plant salt tolerance. *Trends Plant Sci*. 6:2001 66-71.

Zhu JK. *Plant salt stress*. In Encylcopedia of Life Sciences. John Wiley and Sons, Ltd. 2007.

In: Tunisia
Editor: Eunice Wagner
ISBN: 978-1-53610-061-7
© 2016 Nova Science Publishers, Inc.

Chapter 2

COMBINING FAO-56 WITH AN ECONOMIC MODEL TO ASSESS DEFICIT IRRIGATION OF MODERATE SENSIBLE CROP FOR WATER STRESS UNDER SEMI ARID CLIMATE

Hiba Ghazouani[1,*], Amel BelHaj Mguidiche[1], Boutheina Douh M'hamdi[1], Besma Latrach[1], Issam Ghazouani[2] and Abdelhamid Boujelben [1]

[1]Institut Supérieur Agronomique Chott-Meriem, Sousse, Tunisie
[2]Commissariat Régional au Développement Agricole de Jendouba, Tunisie

ABSTRACT

In Tunisia, the expansion of irrigated area and the semiarid climate make it compulsory to adopt strategies of water management to increase water use efficiency. Subsurface drip irrigation (SDI), providing the application of high frequency small irrigation volumes below the soil surface have been increasingly used to enhance irrigation efficiency. Deficit irrigation has shown successful results with a large number of crops in various countries.

Objective of this paper was to assess the effects of deficit irrigation on gross margin and water use efficiency of potatoes crop, irrigated with subsurface drip irrigation, in a semiarid area of central Tunisia. After

* Corresponding author: Hiba Ghazouani. E-mail: ghazouani_hibaunipaisa@yahoo.com.

assessing the validity of FAO-56 spreadsheet program to well simulate soil water status in the root zone, water use efficiency (WUE) was evaluated based on crop yield and simulated actual evapotranspiration. At the same time, irrigation water use efficiency (IWUE) was determined as the ration between crop yield and the amount of water supply to the crop (irrigation).

Field experiments, were carried out in Central Tunisia (10 ◦ 33' 47.0" E, 35 ◦ 58' 8.1 ◦ N, 19 m a.s.l) on a potatoes crop planted in a sandy loam soil, during the growing season 2014, from 15 January to 6 May. Soil water status was monitored in two plots (T1 and T2) maintained under the same management, except for irrigation volumes, provided by a SDI system. More particular, irrigation was scheduled according to the average water content measured in the root zone, with a total of 8 watering, with timing ranging between one and three hours in T1, and between about half-an-hour and one-hour and a-half, in T2. FAO-56 was validated according the average soil water content in all tubes and all observation depths with RMSE values, equal to 0.012 cm^3cm^{-3} and 0.028 cm^3cm^{-3}, respectively for T1 and T2. Simulated actual evapotranspiration in T1 was equal to the potential evapotranspiration. However, it resulted lower than potential evapotranspiration. WUE resulted equal to 32 Kg/m^3 and 16 Kg/m^3, whereas IWUE was equal to 31.7 Kg/m^3 and 45.70 Kg/m^3 for treatments T1 and T2. In terms of gross margin, T1 were more efficient than T2. This finding is directly related to sheep price of water, although its scarcity.

The experimental results and model simulations provided useful guidelines for a more sustainable use of irrigation water.

Keywords: FAO-56, economic model, deficit irrigation, semi arid, gross margin

INTRODUCTION

Potato (Solanum Tuberosum L.) is an essential crop, especially for developed countries. Deficit irrigation (DI) has shown successful results with a large number of crops in various countries. However, for some crops like potato, DI is difficult to manage due to the rapid effect of water stress on tuber yield (Elderge et al., 1992). For a country like Tunisia; drought is one of the most feared phenomena of the expected climatic change. So that, the quantification of crop water requirements is being more and more compulsory. Knowing the actual transpiration fluxes is important to estimate crop water requirement and suggest new irrigation management strategies to improve water use efficiency. The Food and Agricultural Organization (FAO) of the United Nations Irrigation and Drainage Paper 56 (Allen et al. 1998) provides a Penman Monteith method for estimating reference evapotranspiration from standard weather data, and an accurate procedure for computing actual crop evapotranspiration under non stressed and stressed conditions.

Based on economic and agronomic points of view, the term WUE, generally identified by the ratio between the marketable yield and the seasonal values of actual evapotranspiration, has been used as a suitable tool to assess strategies aimed to improve agricultural water use. When considering irrigation practice, irrigation water use efficiency (IWUE) has been defined as the ratio between actual crop transpiration and irrigation water supplied.

$$WUE = \frac{Yy}{ETa}$$

$$IWUE = \frac{Yy}{I} \quad (1)$$

WUE: water use efficiency (Kg/m^3)
Ey: Marketable yield (Kg/ha)
ET: Evapotranspiration (m^3/ha)
IWUE: Irrigation water use efficiency (Kg/m^3)
I: Amount of irrigation (mm)

Doorenbos and Kassam (1979) a proposed a linear function showing a relation between yield response and relative crop evapotranspiration. Joined with the concept of deficit irrigation, water production function allows determining the fall in yield as a result of each level of deficiency in water consumption (Ayas and Korukçu, 2010). An economic model taking into account the price of water and the unit price of yield, allows in to analyse the evolution of the gross profits under the examined scenarios and to define therefore the best irrigation scenario. The gross profits could be expressed as:

$$G = (Y \times Py) - (Wa \times Pw) - (Fa \times Pf) \quad (2)$$

where

G: Gross margin

Y: Obtained yield (t.ha)
Py: Price of unit of yield (TND/t)
Wa: Volume of applied water (m^3/ha)
Pw: Price of unit of water (TND/m^3)
Fa: Amount of fertilizer (Kg/ha)
Pf: Price of unit of fertilizer (TND/Kg)

With these background considerations, a comprehensive field and simulation investigations have been carried out under the semi-arid Tunisian climate. The main objective of this paper is to combine model simulations with a crop productive function and an economic model to choose optimum irrigation dose. Firstly, the ability of the model to predict soil water content has been carried out. Once the model is validated, it was used to calculate, under the elaborated scenarios, the evolution of actual evaporation and transpiration. This allows, by considering a productive function, to study the effect of reducing water supply on the yield fall. Finally, based on an economic model allowing calculating the gross margin, it will be possible to determine the optimum irrigation dose.

The main objective of this paper was to assess the effects of deficit irrigation on water use efficiency of potatoes crop, irrigated with subsurface drip irrigation, in a semiarid area of central Tunisia.

MATERIALS AND METHODS

Experimental Field

The experimental field were laid out in a design block at the experimental field of the high agronomic institute of Chott Mariem, Sousse, Tunisia (Long. 10.5632° N; Lat. 35.9191° N, Altitude 19 m above sea level), consisting of two different irrigation levels. Each plot received the same plant management and was irrigated by a subsurface drip irrigation system (SDI). SDI lateral lines were installed 25 cm bellow the soil surface. The dripper was inline type and placed 0.4 m from each other and delivered 4 l/h flow rate at 1.0 atm pressure. Counters were placed in order to determine the exact water depth that has been provided for the plant. Irrigation amount for full irrigation (T1) were calculated based on common management of the planting area. The water amounts of the other treatment were calculated by using a percentage of deficit

(50%) according to the water amount provided for (T1) treatment. The dominant soil is sandy loam (clay = 8%, silt = 31% and sand = 61%) with an average bulk density of 1.6 g.cm^{-3} for a layer thickness of 80 cm. Basic seed tubers of Potato crop 'SolanumTuberosum L.,' cultivar Safran were planted with a distance of 40 cm along the row and 80 cm between the row. Soil water content was daily monitored at 10, 25 and 50 cm from the emitter using a potable 'Trime FM' probe that had been previously calibrated by Ghazouani et al. (2015). The site specific calibration showed a precision of ± 0.03 cm^3/cm^3 for the obtained soil moisture measurements. In each experimental plot and immediately after planting, three access tubes were placed at 5, 25 and 50 cm from the emitter in a perpendicular direction to the plant row.

Statistical Analysis for Model Evaluation

The performance of FAO-56 model was evaluated by considering the Mean Bias Error (MBE), Root Mean Square Error (RMSE), and Nash-Sutcliffe model efficiency coefficient (E) (Nash and Sutcliffe, 1970; Willmott, 1981).

$$MBE = \frac{1}{N}\sum_{i=1}^{N}(X_{sim,i} - X_{obs,i}) \tag{3}$$

$$RMSE = \sqrt{\frac{\sum_{i=1}^{N}(X_{sim,i} - X_{obs,i})^2}{N}} \tag{4}$$

$$E = 1 - \frac{\sum_{i=1}^{N}(X_{sim,i} - X_{obs,i})^2}{\sum_{i=1}^{N}(X_{obs,i} - \overline{X_{obs}})^2} \tag{5}$$

where $X_{sim,i}$ and $X_{obs,i}$ represent the simulated and observed values of the considered variable at the time i and N the number of measured data.

RESULTS

Validation of FAO 56 Model on the Base of Measured Soil Water Content

The comparison between measured and simulated soil water contents for treatments T1 and T2 is illustrated in Figure 1a and Figure 1b, respectively. As can be observed, FAO-56 model is able to reproduce the evolution of the average soil water content. Table 1 shows the values of *MBE*, *RMSE* and Nash efficiency index, *E*, evaluated for treatments T1 and T2. From that table, it is confirmed that FAO-56 model is able to simulate quite accurately the soil water content distribution around a buried emitter.

The shift between simulated and measured soil water content, visible in Figure 1.a-b, especially, for treatment T2 could be ascribed to a possible air gaps formation, near the soil surface, between the access tube and the surrounding soil. Moreover, for both the treatments, simulated values varied with the range variation of the square error of the average measured soil water content. A slight decrease of soil water content can be observed from the starting of growing season till roughly DOY 70 (crop at full development stage), after that a quick decline occurred, as a consequence of the relatively high potential crop evapotranspiration in that period.

Water Use Efficiency and Gross Margin

After Assessing FAO-56 Model to evaluate the effect of deficit irrigation on actual evapotranspiration. Water Use Efficiency WUE and Irrigation Water Use Efficiency IWUE were evaluated. WUE resulted equal to 32 Kg/m^3 and 16 Kg/m^3, whereas IWUE was equal to 31.7 Kg/m^3 and 45.70 Kg/m^3 for treatments T1 and T2, respectively. The higher IWUE obtained in T2 respect to T1, is a direct consequence of the lower irrigation volumes provided to the crop. The significant difference on yield between T1 (39.4 ± 2.3 t/ha) and T2 (27.94 ± 1.07 t/ha) confirms the assumption that potato crop extract water as much as it is available in the root zone and starting from the wetter region with lower matric potential passing than to the drier ones (Homaee et al., 2002).

Table 1. Statistical comparisons between simulated and average measured soil water contents

MBE	0.002	0.02
RMSE	0.012	0.028
E	0.842	0.749

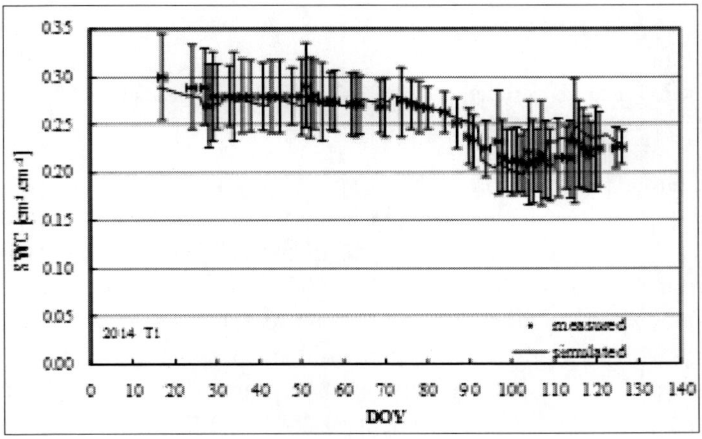

a

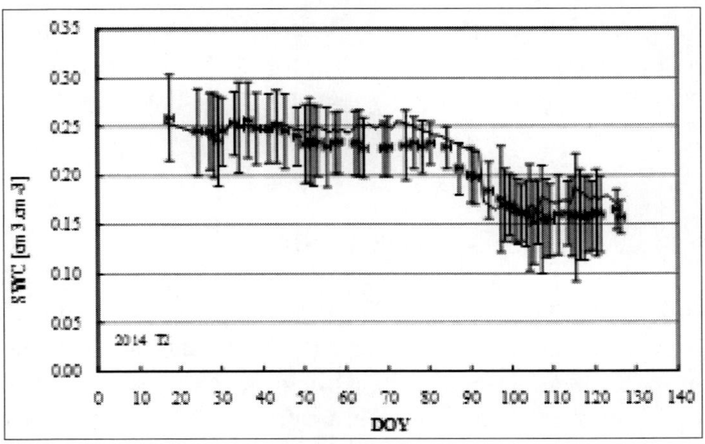

b

Figure 1. (a-b) Comparison average measured (black dots) and simulated (solid line) soil water content during the growing season for T1 (a) and T2 (b).

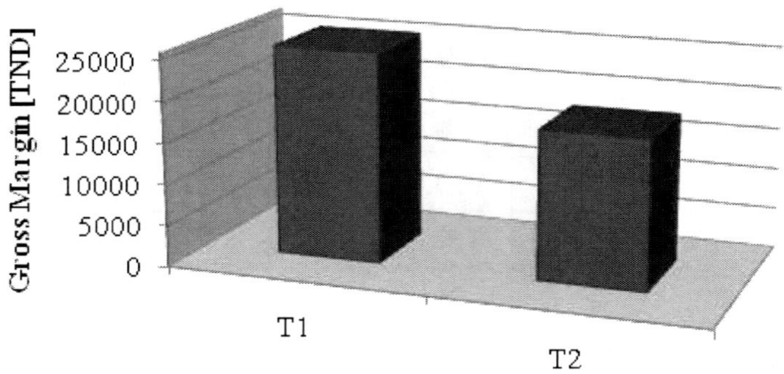

Figure 2. Gross margin as function of irrigation dose for both treatment T1 and T2.

The Gross margin (G) for the different scenario was calculated based on equation (1). According to the Tunisian ministry of commerce (2016), the price of potatoes was considered equal to 650 TND/t. The price of 1 m^3 of water from the dam was equal to 0.120 TND. Potatoes crop were grow up without any fertilization application for that reason, costs of nitrogen fertilizer were not involved in that calculation. Results in terms of gross margin show a significant difference between both treatments Figure 2. In fact, T1 presented a higher gross margin which was equal to 25460 TND vs 18061 TND for T2. These findings are on harmony with the ones obtained by El Amami et al. (2001) who studied the effect of Deficit Irrigation on Cereals and Horticultural Crops by the mean of Economic Analysis. They found that under no water restriction, optimal irrigation strategy is achieved when providing for the plant its whole water need.

Conclusion

FAO-56 spreadsheet was used for potato crop ('SolanumTuberosum L.') irrigated by a subsurface drip irrigation system during the experimental campaign of 2014 in the semi-arid environment of the central Tunisia. Field experiments aimed to test two different treatments (T1; T2) maintained under the same management, except for irrigation depth. Firstly, FAO-56 was validated according the average soil water content in all tubes and observation depths. WUE resulted equal to 32 Kg/m^3 and 16 Kg/m^3, whereas IWUE was equal to 31.7 Kg/m^3 and 45.70 Kg/m^3 for treatments T1 and T2, respectively.

The experimental results, joined to model simulations suggested the treatment T1 as an irrigation strategy for a more sustainable use of irrigation water in the central Tunisia. However, under a strong condition of water shortage, the price of water should rise and the optimal irrigation strategy will be T2.

REFERENCES

Allen, R. G., Periera, L. S., Raes, D., and Smith, M. 1998. Crop evapotranspiration: Guidelines for computing crop requirements, irrigation and drainage. *FAO Paper No. 56*, Food and Agricultural Organization, Rome, 300.

Ayas, S. and A. Korukcu, 2010. Water-yield relationships in deficit irrigated potato. *Journal of Agricultural Faculty of Uludag University*, 24 (2): 23-36.

Doorenbos, J. and Kassam, A.H. 1979. Yield response to water. *FAO Irrigation and Drainage Paper No. 33*. Rome, FAO.

El Amami, H., A. Zairi, L. S. Pereira, T. Machado, A. Slatni, and P. Rodrigues. March 2001. “Deficit Irrigation of Cereals and Horticultural Crops: Economic Analysis.” Agricultural Engineering International: the CIGR Journal of Scientific Research and Development. *Manuscript LW 00 007b*. Vol. III.

Eldredge, E.P., Shock, C.C. andStieber, T.D. 1992. Plot sprinklers for irrigation research. *Agronomy Journal* 84: 1081-1084.

Homaee M., Feddes R.A., Dirksen C. 2002. Simulation of root water uptake: II Non-uniform transient water stress using different reduction functions. *Agricultural Water Management*, 57, 111-126.

Ghazouani H., Douh B., Autovino D., Mguidiche A., Rallo G., Provenzano G. and BoujelbenA. 2015. Optimizing Subsurface Dripline Installation depth with Hydrus 2D/3D to improve irrigation water Use efficiency in the central Tunisia. *International Journal of Metrology and Quality*, 6(4), 402-432.

Nash, J. E. and Sutcliffe, J. V.: River flow forecasting through conceptual models, Part I - A discussion of principles, *Journal of Hydrology*, 10, 282-290, 1970.

Willmott C.J.: On the validation of models, *Physical geography*, 2, 184-194, 1981.

BIOGRAPHICAL SKETCH

Ghazouani Hiba

Affiliation:
Institut Supérieur Agronomique Chott-Meriem, Sousse, Tunisie.

Education: PhD student (Soil water environment)

Publications Last 3 Years:

H. Ghazouani, D. Autovino, B. Douh, A. Boujlben, G. Provenzano, G. Rallo. 2014. Using Hydrus 2-D to assess the emitters optimal position for Eggplants under surface and subsurface drip irrigation. *Paper 2014-3151.* European Geoscience Union General Assembly, Vienna, Austria, 27 April - 02 May.

Hiba Ghazouani, Giuseppe Provenzano, Giovanni Rallo, Amel Mguidiche, Boutheina Douh and Abdelhamid Boujelben, 2015. Irrigation management strategies to improve Water Use Efficiency of potatoes crop in Central Tunisia. *Paper 2014-2886.* European Geoscience Union General Assembly, Vienna, Austria, 12 April – 17 April.

Ghazouani Hiba, Douh Boutheina,Giuseppe Provenzano, Giovanni Rallo, Dario Autovino, Mguidich Amel et Boujelben Abdelhamid. Optimizing Subsurface Drip installation depth with Hydrus 2D/3D to improve irrigation water use efficiency in the central Tunisia. Monastir, Tunisia.

Hiba Ghazouani, Dario Autovino, Giovanni Rallo, Boutheina Douh and Giuseppe Provenzano. 2015. Using HYDRUS-2D model to assess the optimal drip lateral depth for Eggplant crop in a sandy loam soil of central Tunisia. *Italian Journal of Agrometeorology.*

Giuseppe Provenzano, Giovanni Rallo, Hiba Ghazouani. 2015. Assessing field and laboratory calibration protocols for the Diviner2000 probe in a range of soils with different texture. *Journal Irrigation and Drainage Engineering.*

In: Tunisia
Editor: Eunice Wagner
ISBN: 978-1-53610-061-7
© 2016 Nova Science Publishers, Inc.

Chapter 3

Performance Evaluation of AquaCrop in Simulating Soil Water Content, Canopy Cover, and Root Development for Maize Conducted under Subsurface Drip Irrigation

Boutheina Douh M'hamdi*[1,*]*, Nada Abdelkader*[2]*,
Amel Mguidich Bel Haj*[1]*, Hiba Ghazouani*[1]*, Sami Khila*[1]
***and Abdelhamid Boujelben*[1]**
[1]Height Agronomic Institute of Chott Meriem,
University of Sousse, Sousse, Tunisia
[2]CIHEAM IAMM, University of Montpelier, Montpelier, France

Abstract

In this study, AquaCrop model was evaluated for maize (*Zea mays* L.) in the experimental site of Chott Mariem, Sousse (semi-arid climate), with data from two companions corn grown in the years 2008 and 2010. The crop was led under subsurface drip irrigation (SDI) to 20 cm deep. The simulation was repeatedly made on three parameters to know soil water content (SWC), canopy cover and root development. The best wedging SWC belonged to statistical estimators values ranging from 1.1

[*] E-mail: boutheina_douh@yahoo.fr.

to 3.34 for the RMSE, between [0-1] for R^2 and efficiency EF (often positive) values very close to zero for the CRM (-0.001 for the water content to 20 cm depth), and a ≈ 1 CD. Concerning the canopy cover calibration, the wedging settled with R^2 in the range of 0.92 seen fit enough (the ideal is $R^2 = 1$), and root development was rigged with a RMSE in the range of 3.13, an $R^2 = 0.92$, a CRM, CD and EF in the desired standards. Although the quality of the calibration for all three parameters was considered good enough through graphics and estimators calculated, validation, concerning only the water content and root development, gave a perfect complement to only the root growth ($R^2 = 0.99$). The validation of the moisture content with data of the partner 2008, indeed gave negative values of the efficiency EF in the majority of the depths, so showing that the experimental values are better than those feigned. This regression of the quality of validation was, according to us, the result of the various defects of the model to know the not consideration of the depth of the subsurface drip irrigation system, the conservatives parameters are not precise for a specific range and the fixation of the own percentages in sand, silt and clay by the user, is not possible.

Keywords: AquaCrop, SDI, SWC, canopy cover, root development, RMSE

INTRODUCTION

The sustainability of agricultural production depend on conservation and appropriate use and management of scarce water resources especially in arid and semi-arid region, where irrigation is required for the production of food (Douh and Boujelben, 2011). Grain corn (*Zea mays* L.) is sensitive to soil water availability, which can be influenced by irrigation application method. Subsurface drip irrigation (SDI) minimize adverse environmental consequence of irrigation and reduce evaporative losses from the soil surface. Further, deficit irrigation may be practiced with less risk using SDI (Douh et al. 2013, Mguidich et al. 2014, El Mokh et al., 2014; Ghazouani et al., 2015). To use such strategies effectively, it will be necessary to develop a good understanding of crops' responses to water stress along with tools for modeling responses to water deficits and other environmental factors. Although deficit irrigation involves subjecting crops to water stress and would thus be expected to depress yields, it is possible to maintain good yields by ensuring that sufficient water is supplied during critical stages of crop growth and only imposing water stress during growth stages that can tolerate it (Geerts and Raes, 2009). Models make it possible to evaluate the effects of different yield-affecting factors simultaneously in order to identify optimal irrigation regimes for specific scenarios (Liu et al., 2007; Pereira et al., 2002). The newly AquaCrop model was developed by the FAO (Food and Agricultural Organization) to simulate yield responses to changes in the supply of water (Xiangxiang et al., 2013). It's free and practitioner oriented for the users, and requires a relatively small number of parameters to calculate the yield and biomass. As it aims at maintaining a balance between accuracy, robustness (Raes et al., 2009; Steduto et al., 2009). However, the model has not been tested in the central of Tunisia where crop yields is often limited by water availability. In the light of the above this study was initiated among other things to assess evaluate and validate the AquaCrop model by using it to simulate soil water content, canopy cover, and root development for maize conducted under subsurface drip irrigation.

MATERIALS AND METHODS

Study Area

The data used in this work were collected between 2008 and 2010. The experiment was carried out at the Higher Institute of Agronomy of Chott Meriem, Tunisia with Longitude 10°38' E, Latitude 35°55' N, altitude 15 m (Figure 1).

Climatic Aspects

The climate is typically Mediterranean with 230 mm annual rainfall and an average of 6 mm day-1 evaporation from a free water surface. In winter, the average minimum temperature is 6°C and the average maximum is 18°C, while in summer average minimum is 23°C and average maximum is 38°C (Figure 2). Potential evapotranspiration was calculated by the Penman-Monteith method as outlined by Allen et al. (1998).

Figure 1. Location of field experimental site.

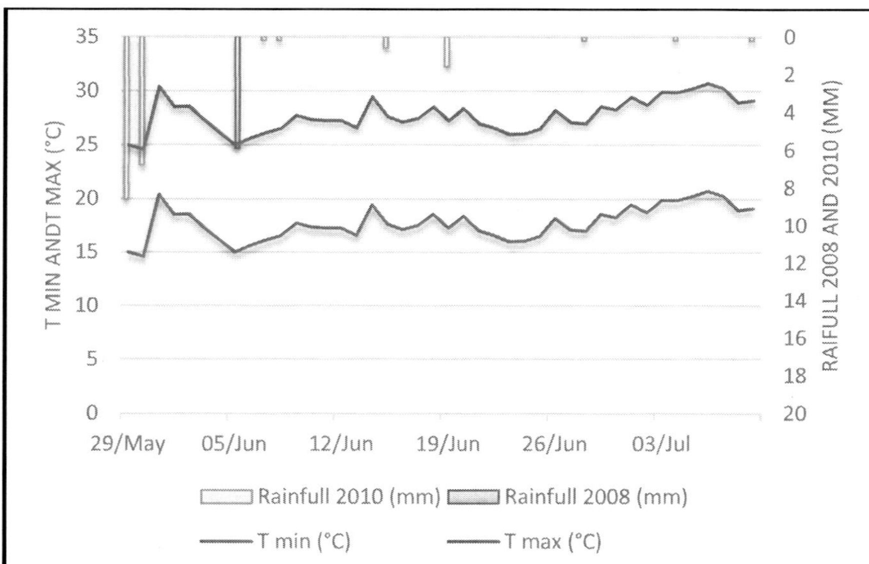

Figure 2. Weather parameters during the crop grown period.

Experimental Trial

The soil is sandy loam with average basic infiltration rate of 14mm h^{-1}. Bulk density of soil was found to be 1.40 g cm^{-3} for the layer 0-60 cm. The field was precision graded to approximately 1 mm m^{-1} slope. Maize (*Zea mays* L.) was seeded the 1st of May with row spacing of 80 cm and in-row spacing of 40 cm and the whole planting area is 1,000 m^2 (25 m × 40 m). The maize crop was irrigated with subsurface drip irrigation (SDI) at 20 cm depth during the growing season. Drip tubing (GR type, 16 mm diameter) with 40 cm emitter were used. TDR *"Trime Fm"* was used to measure water content daily (Figure 3).

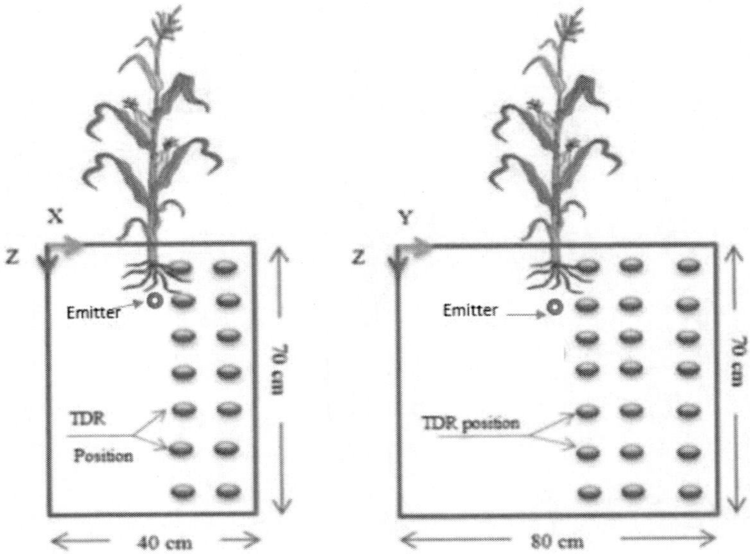

Figure 3. Experimental layout.

AquaCrop Evaluation

The two years of experimental results were used to validate the AquaCrop model for the site while the climate data were used to simulate water content and root length. Some parameters that resemble those during experimental periods were adjusted as suggested by Hsiao et al. (2009).

Model Evaluation

AquaCrop model simulation results of maize parameters were compared with the observed values form the experiment during both calibration and validation processes. The goodness of fit between the simulated and observed values was corroborated by using the prediction error statistics. The coefficient of determination (R^2), root mean square error (RMSE) and model efficiency (Ef) were used as the error statistics to evaluate validation results of the model. The R^2 and Ef were used to access the predictive power of the model while the CRM and RMSE indicated the error in model prediction. The following statistical indicators were used to compare the measured and simulated values. Model performance was evaluated using the following statistical parameters (Nash and Sutcliffe, 1970), given by:

$$RMSE = \sqrt{\frac{1}{n}\sum_1^n (P_i - O_i)^2}$$

$$EF = \frac{\sum_{i=1}^n (O_i - \bar{O})^2 - \sum_{i=1}^n (P_i - O_i)^2}{\sum_1^n (O_i - \bar{O})^2}$$

$$R^2 = \left[\frac{\sum_{i=1}^n (O_i - \bar{O})(P_i - \bar{P})}{\sqrt{\sum_{i=1}^n (O_i - \bar{O})^2}\sqrt{\sum_{i=1}^n (P_i - \bar{P})^2}}\right]^2$$

$$\mathrm{CRM} = \frac{\sum_1^n O_i - \sum_1^n P_i}{\sum_1^n O_i}$$

$$CD = \frac{\sum_1^n (O_i - \bar{O})^2}{\sum_1^n (P_i - \bar{O})^2}$$

Model efficiency (Ef); CD and R^2 approaching one and P, CRM and RMSE close to zero were indicators for better model performance.

RESULTS AND DISCUSSION

Figure 4 shows the water content observed and simulated respectively for 10, 20, 30, 40, 50 60 and 70 cm depth.

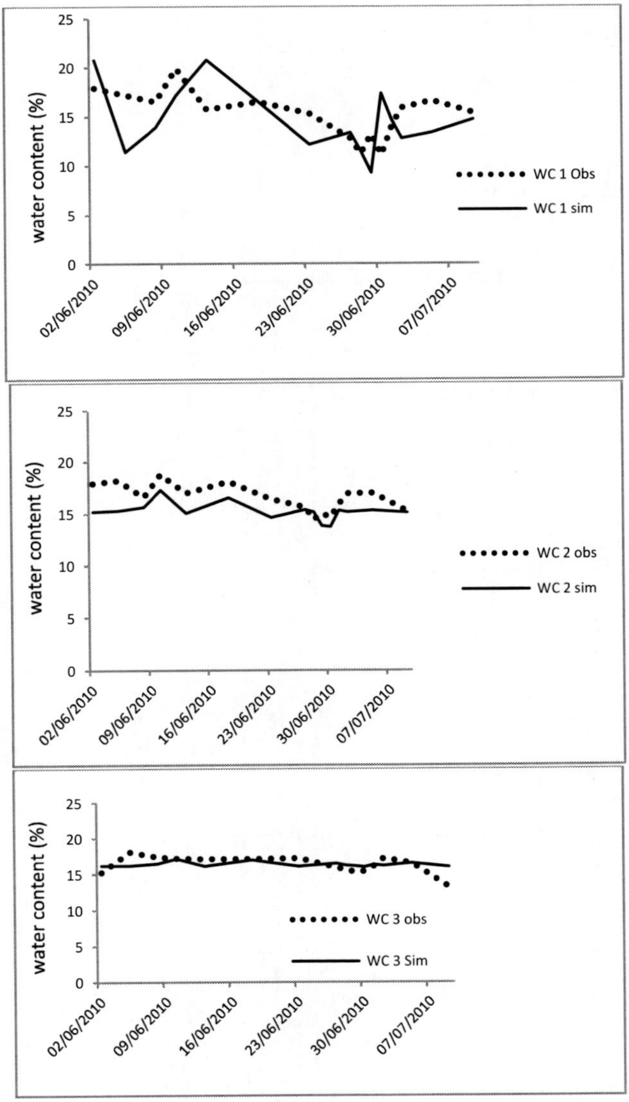

Figure 4. (Continued)

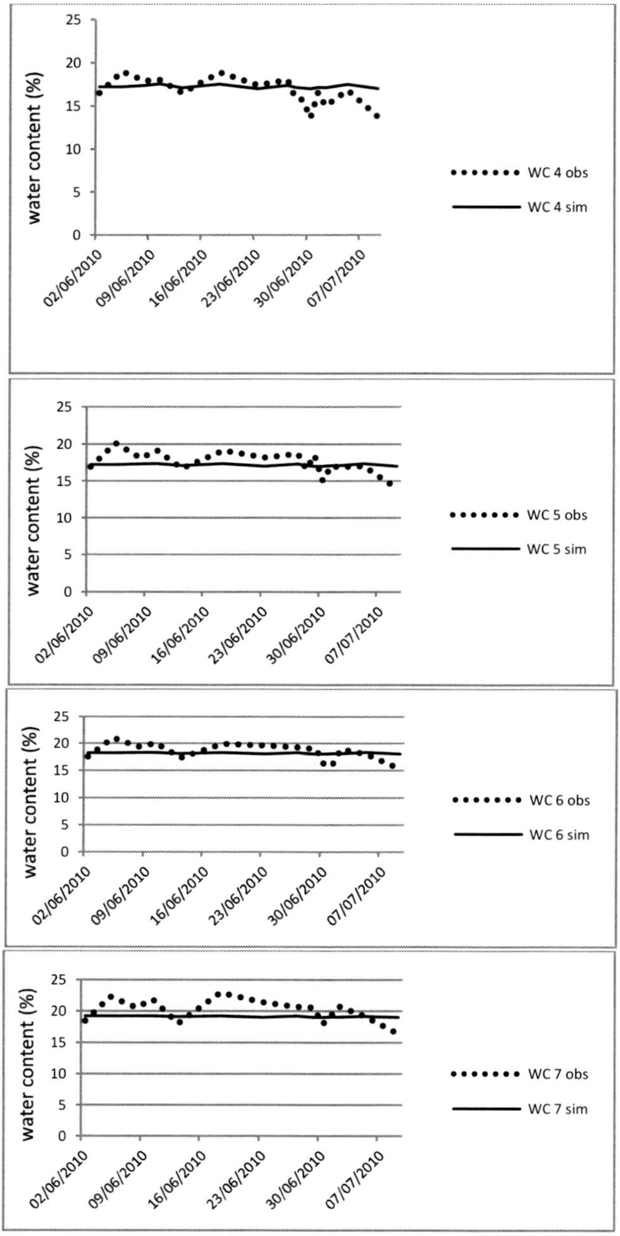

Figure 4. Water content observed and simulated at 10, 20, 30, 40, 50 60 and 70 cm depth.

Table 1. Values of statistical estimator's evaluation water contents at different depths

	RMSE	EF	R^2	CRM	CD
WC1	3,341905	-1,008115	0,115150	0,041012	0,497979
WC2	1,581033	-0,41440	0,5073655	0,041012	0,707009
WC3	1,104611	0,141104	0,1540831	-0,001022	1,164285
WC4	1,593894	0,013099	0,476396	-0,034669	1,013273
WC5	1,516520	0,050074	0,298729	0,016991	1,052713
WC6	1,582403	0,030459	0,216519	0,014130	1,031416
WC7	1,961759	-0,242057	0,206240	0,046724	0,805115

The evaluating of the model performance with calculation of the statistical estimators also certified that good fit: the RMSE ranged from [12.69 to 21.35] before calibration to a range [1.1 to 3.34] after calibration (plus RMSE is closed to zero more calibration is robust). This field variation of the value of RMSE is better than that found by Ngetich and colleagues (2012) for wedging the water content performed at depths of 0-15cm, 15-25cm and 25-35cm. In fact, this setting of the water content of the soil for two experimental sites Kenya gave the RMSE values varying in the range [2.23 to 13.29]. The efficiency EF scored four positive values indicating that the simulated values are better than those observed, and varying an interval of [-320.02 to -27.94] before calibration at an interval close to [0-1] after, CRM has given very close to zero values (ideally CRM = 0) and the CD gave values close to 1 (ideally CD = 1), indicating a perfect match with the observed data. The following table summarizes all statistical estimators calculated values for different soil depths WC1 ... WC7 = moisture respectively depth 10cm to 70cm deep (Table 1).

Validation is done keeping the same .CRO extension file belonging to the calibration parameters of the campaign 2010. Other input data belongs to the 2008 campaign as mentioned earlier. The level validation root development showed a better deal compared to the results of the timing at this level (Figure 5). Indeed, the cloud points focused on the bisecting line Y = X, indicating a very good agreement and conformity between the observed and simulated ones. The adjustment Goodness of fit R^2 confirmed this similarity with a percentage very close to 1 (R^2 = 0.996). Which confirms the agreement between the observed and the simulated values, given the rapprochement of the two curves and their intersection at the end of the simulation period.

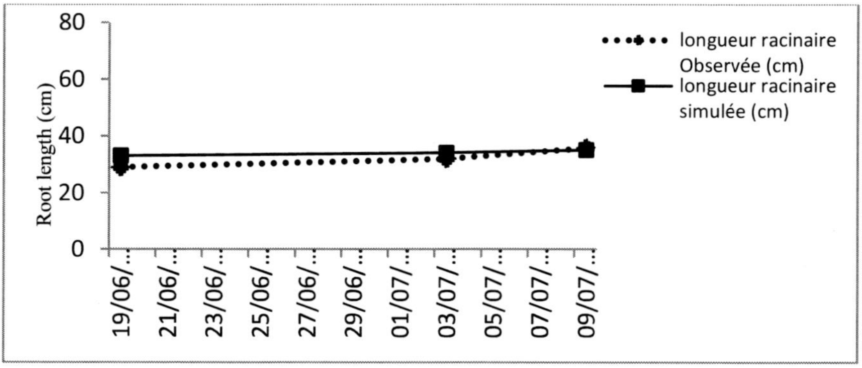

Figure 5. Comparison of simulated and observed root lengths.

CONCLUSION

The AquaCrop model can be used to model the impact of different irrigation regimes on semi-arid climate such as Tunisia. The model accurately simulates the soil water content of the root zone as well as agronomics parameters. Therefore, it was dedicated to realize the calibration and validation of this model of irrigation management for the evaluation of hydro-Agricultural activities of a corn crop driving under the underground drip irrigation. The parameters involved in the rigging were basically the water content in different depths of soil, green cover and root development of corn. The results were quite satisfactory timing (RMSE not exceeding 3 for the water content, a R^2 between [0-1], a CRM and a $\approx$ 0 CD $\approx$ 1 for all parameters). Validation has also yielded results in the desired standards (R^2 up to 0.996, and a CRM $\approx$ 0) but it could be better (EF $<$ 0 in most validation results) if AquaCrop had not a number of handling faults during the data entry process. Although conservative parameters facilitated the simulation output settings in most cases they are a limiting factor to the specificity of the execution, given the wide range of criteria applicable to several scenarios. Working with such software could solve various problems, mainly in the field of farm management, but the resolution required a large number of input data difficult to collect them all. Thereby creating another program with the same strength but with a number of input parameters smaller seems to be a necessary goal to achieve in view of the development of agricultural progress.

REFERENCES

[1] Allen R.G., L.S. Pereira, D. Raes, M. Smith, 1998. Crop évapotranspiration- Guidelines for computing crop water requirements- FAO irrigation and drainage paper 56.FAO Food and Agriculture Organization of the United Nation, Rome, 15p.

[2] Douh B., A. Boujelben, S. Khila and A. Belhaj Mguidiche, 2013. Effect of subsurface drip irrigation system depth on soil water content distribution at different depths and different times after irrigation, *LARHYSS journal*, 13, pp 7-16.

[3] Douh Boutheina and Abdelhamid Boujelben, 2011. Subsurface drip irrigation and water management under semiarid climate. *Book title: Advances in Environmental Research. Volume 22.* Editors: Justin A. Daniels. ISBN: 978-1-61470-743-1, Edition Nova Publisher, pp.181-198.

[4] El Mokh Fathia, Paul D. Colaizzi, Steven R. Evett[2] and David K. Brauer, 2014. Corn Yield and Water Use Efficiency under Contrasting Irrigation Application Methods: An Aquacrop Study Contrasting Subsurface Drip and Sprinkler Irrigation Methods, conference, ASA-CSSA-SSSA International Annual Meeting, 2-5 Novembre, Long Beach, CA.

[5] Geerts, S., Raes, D., 2009. Deficit irrigation as an on-farm strategy to maximize crop water productivity in dry areas. *Agricultural Water Management 96*, 1275–1284.

[6] Ghazouani Hiba, Boutheina Douh M'hamdi, Dario Autovino, Amel Mguidiche Bel Haj, Giovanni Rallo, Giuseppe Provenzano and Abdelhamid Boujelben, 2015. Optimizing Subsurface Dripline Installation depth with Hydrus 2D/3D to improve irrigation water Use efficiency in the central Tunisia, *Int. J. Metrol. Qual. Eng.* 6, 402, 8p.

[7] Hsiao C.T., H. Lee, P. Steduto, R.L. Basilio, D. Raes et F. Elias, 2009. AquaCrop –The FAO Model to simulate Yield Response to water: Parameterisation and testing for Maize. Alliance of Crop, Soil and Environmental Science Scocieties, Article n°20334, PP 448-459.

[8] Liu, J., Wiberg, D., Zehnder, A.J., Yang, H., 2007. Modeling the role of irrigation in winter wheat yield, crop water productivity, and production in China. *Irrigation Science* 26, 21–33.

[9] Mguidich A., B. Douh Mhamdi, S. Bhouri Khila, A. Boujelben, 2014. Subsurface drip irrigation of Potato under Tunisian climatic condition, *Scientia Agriculturae* (SA), 1 (3), 103-109.

[10] Nash, J.E., Sutcliffe, J.V., 1970. River flow forecasting through conceptual models. I. A discussion of principles. *Journal of Hydrology* 10, 282–290.
[11] Ngetich K.F., D. Raes, C.A. Shisanya, J. Mugwe, M. Mucheru-Muna, D.N. Mugendi et J. Diels, 2012. *Calibration and validation of AquaCrop model for maize in Sub-humid and semi-arid regions of central highlands of Kenya. Third* Ruforum Biennial Meeting 24 - 28 September 2012, Entebbe, Uganda, 24p.
[12] Pereira, L.S., Oweis, T., Zairi, A., 2002. Irrigation management under water scarcity. *Agricultural Water Management* 57, 175–206.
[13] Raes, D., Steduto, P., Hsiao, T., Fereres, E., 2009. Aquacrop Reference Manual. FAO – Land and Water Division, Rome, Italy.
[14] Steduto, P., Hsiao, T.C., Raes, D., Fereres, E., 2009. AquaCrop – the FAO crop model to simulate yield response to water: I. Concepts and underlying principles. *Agronomy Journal* 101, 426–437.
[15] Xiangxiang Wang, Wang Quanjiu, Fan Jun and Fu Qiuping, 2013. Evaluation of the AquaCrop model for simulating the impact of water deficits and different irrigation regimes on the biomass and yield of winter wheat grown on China's Loess Plateau, *Agricultural Water Management,* Volume 129, Pages 95–104.

In: Tunisia
Editor: Eunice Wagner
ISBN: 978-1-53610-061-7
© 2016 Nova Science Publishers, Inc.

Chapter 4

THERMAL PERFORMANCES AND ECONOMIC ANALYSIS OF SOLAR WATER HEATING SYSTEMS FEASIBILITY FOR DOMESTIC APPLICATIONS IN TUNISIA

Majdi Hazami*, Nabiha Naili, Issam Attar and Abdelhamid Farhat
Laboratoire des Procédées Thermiques,
Centre de Recherche et des Technologies de l'Energie, Borj-Cedria
Hammam-Lif, Tunis, Tunisia

ABSTRACT

This paper presents new angles on analyzing Domestic Solar Water Heating systems (DSWHs) deployment in Tunisia by analyzing both the energetic and the economic potential through a case study related to Tunisian scenario. In this scenario we evaluate the performance and the life cycle perspective of the two most popular DSWHs over the recent years (i.e., DSWH with flat-plate solar collector, installation No. 1, and DSWHs with evacuated-tube solar collector, installation No. 2). The dynamic behavior of DSWHs according to Tunisian data weather is achieved by means of TRNSYS simulation. Results show that the

---

* Corresponding author: Tel 71430044 / 71430215, Fax: 71430934. E-mail: Hazamdi321@yahoo.fr.

installations No. 1 and No. 2 supplies 1555.38 kWh/year and 1618.75 kWh/ year of energy. Using estimates from the demand-side of hot water for a typical Tunisian household composed of 4-5 persons, the paper evaluates the economic potential of DSWHs in saving electricity and reducing carbon dioxide emissions. Results show that the annual savings in electrical energy and payback period relatively to the No. 1, were 1316 kWh/year and 8 years based on electric water heater, or 306 m3 gas saving and 6 years payback period based on gas water heater, respectively. For the installation No. 2 the annual electricity saving and payback period were 1459 kWh/year and 10 years based on electric water heater, or 410 m3gas saving and 7.5 years payback period based on gas water heater, respectively. The life cycle savings by installing the solar system instead of buying electricity/gas/town gas to satisfy hot water needs is about 3969 $ (Installation No. 1) and 4400.34 $ (Installation No. 2) for electricity backup and is about 1517.76 $ (Installation No. 1) and 2035.24 $ (Installation No. 2) for gas/town gas backup. From an environmental point of view the annual GHG emission per house is reduced by 27800 tCO2.

Keywords: DSWH system, energy consumption, energy payback, energy return

NOMENCLATURE

c_1	first order efficiency coefficient, $kJ.h^{-1}m^{-2}K^{-1}$
c_2	second order efficiency coefficient, $kJ.h^{-1}m^{-2}K^{-2}$
C_p	specific heat capacity, $kJ.m^{-2}\ K^{-1}$
DSWH	domestic solar water heating
f	solar fraction, %
G	solar radiation, $W.m^{-2}$
K_θ	Incidence Angle Modified (IAM)
Q_{Aux}	auxiliary energy supplied to the system, *kWh*
Q_C	heat collected by solar collector, *kWh*
Q_{Ext}	annual energy extracted, *kWh*
Q_I	the total radiation incident on the collector, $kWh.m^{-2}$
Q_{lost}	annual energy lost, *kWh*
T_{ext}	ambient air temperature, *K*
T_i	temperature at the beginning of the test, *K*
T_{in}	water inlet temperature of solar collector, *K*
T_f	temperature at the end of the test (After 24 h), *K*

T_m	mean water temperature a cross the solar collector, *K*
T_{out}	water outlet temperature of solar collector, *K*
T_S	mean water temperature inside the hot water storage c ylinder, *K*
U_c	heat loss coefficient of the hot water cylinder storage $W.m^{-2}.K^{-1}$
V	volume of the water in the storage tank, m^3

Greek symbols

η	thermal efficiency, %
η_0	intercept efficiency, %

1. Introduction

Tunisia is a small country of 162 155 km², located at the northern most part of Africa. It is bordered on the west by Algeria and on the south by Libya and the Mediterranean sea to the northeast and north with a 1300 km of coastline (Figure 1). It lies between latitudes 30° and 38°N, and longitudes 7° and 12°E. Despite its small size, Tunisia offers a remarkably diverse natural landscape. The country is divided into three distinct physical regions, the Tell Atlas Mountains and the Dorsale Ridge separated by the fertile valley of the Medjerda River in the north. Tunisia has a temperate Mediterranean climate characterized by warm dry summers and wet winters influenced by sea breezes [1].

Despite limited hydrocarbon resources, Tunisia has enjoyed a promising energy situation characterized by a largely surplus energy balance until the middle of the Eighties. The energy sector played during this period a key role in financing the economic growth of the country, representing in 1980 approximately 13% of the national GDP and 16% of the national exports [2]. The contribution of the energy sector in the economic growth has been decreasing since 1986. Currently, the energy sector accounts for approximately 5% of the GDP of the country and less than 7% of the total national exports. Since the end of the Eighties, the favorable situation started to deteriorate due to the joint effect of two major factors which are: (i) The stagnation of the national hydrocarbon resources and (ii) The sharp increase of energy demand, notably electricity, as induced by economic and social growth [3]. Thus, the energy balance moved from a surplus situation of approximately 3Mtoe in the beginning of the Eighties to a slightly deficit situation starting early year 2000. In order to address this deficit, the Tunisian authorities have engaged an energy policy that is compatible with sustainable development. The main component is the intensification and reinforcement of the efforts made for the development of the country's hydrocarbon resources including an extension of exploration activities. In 2003, Tunisian's imports of oil reached 128.3 million tones, or around 46% of oil consumption, following growing energy demand and supply imbalances [4]. Today, following two decades of economic growth and rising demand for energy products, Tunisian's citizens are becoming more environmentally aware. The concerns related to improving the energy balance has also led the public authorities to set in October 2000 a National Energy Efficiency and Renewable Energies Commission whose missions included in particular the drawing up of a national program aimed at rationalizing energy consumption and promoting renewable energies [5, 6].

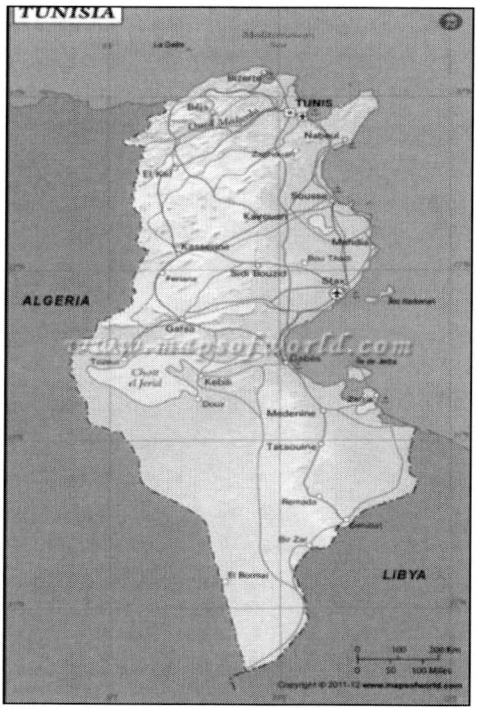

Figure 1. Tunisia geographic situation.

As a result, Tunisian policy makers have begun acknowledging the need to resort to cleaner sources of energy, particularly solar energy mainly used for domestic water heating purposes.In fact, the country is blessed with a huge amount of solar energy which ranges from 1800 kWh/m² per year in the North to 2600kWh/m² per year in the South spread over 3000 hours. This favorable circumstance allows Tunisia to be a pioneer in the exploitation of solar energy in the production of domestic hot water at a temperature around 50–60 °C which can be meet easily by means of DSWH systems [7, 8]. Thus considerable efforts have been made by Tunisian government towards the development and the dissemination of DSWH systems which offers a significant contribution in the reducing of electricity demand, energy expenditure and saving the environment from gas emission. From the other side, the installation of these systems will create employment due to the use of locally manufactured solar water heaters and savings in the cost of energy. Accordingly, a demonstration program during the 1980’s was launched for promoting DSWH systems in the country by offering to the end users a variety of financial and fiscal incentives (ANME, 2007). These include capital subsidy, low interest loan, accelerated depreciation related benefit etc. Under this program several DSWHs were installed. The widely commercialized of these DSWH systems in Tunisia are the conventional forced circulation type or the thermo-siphon type based on flat-plate collectors and water storage tank used in Tunisia since 1950 and present about 30% of the installed systems [8]. Recently a new DSWH systems based on evacuated tube collector has been introduced in Tunisian market. The dissemination of these kinds of DSWH systems in requires necessarily the evaluation of the long-term efficiency quite to Tunisian climates, the economic feasibility, the initial cost and the payback period. In the most of published papers the long-term efficiency of DSWH systems is evaluated by determining the monthly or even annual energy supplied the solar fraction and the thermal efficiencies. For example, Crawford et al. [9], Tsilingiridis et al. [10] and Rey-Martinez et al. [11] adopted a simulation method to calculate the annual solar fraction and the annual energy supplied to the end users to evaluate the energy consumed by DSWH systems and to appraise the economic feasibility of the DSWH systems. This last is evaluated through the determination of the energy saving (AES), the payback assessment (EP) and the energy return (ER) which are to date the most widely used tools for generating the environmental profile of the DSWH systems [12, 13, 14]. A literature search on AES, EP and ER of DSWH systems shows that most of the research reported is for European scenarios, and the cases for African or Arab country are rare. This paper investigates the potential of

DSWH systems in alleviating energy and environmental benefits in Tunisia by making a comparative evaluation of water heating practices in the domestic sector. A scenario through a case study in Borjcedria, Tunis, Tunisia (36° 379 N to 42° 029 N), representing mild and hot climates is achieved for two installations (DSWH system based on flat-plate solar collector, No. 1, and DSWH system based on evacuated tubes solar collector, No. 2). The economic benefits that accrue from using DSWHs are then opposed to conventional water heating technologies (electric and gas:/town gas heater) tocompare their performance according to Tunisian scenarios. The study is achieved by means of the TRNSYS computer simulation model [15]. Then a generalization analyses to all Tunisia is achieved.

2. Energy in Tunisia

2.1. Tunisian Energy Production and Consumption

Tunisian's country has a population of about 10.6 million of which 65% live in urban areas and 35% are in rural areas [16]. There are about 1.02 million urban households and 2.04 million rural households. On average, Tunisian household's has about 4.21 persons with a national population grown at about 1.2% per year. About 96% of the population is connected to the national grid [17]. According to the International Energy Agency, the total primary energy production in Tunisia (7.9 Mtoe) is mainly driven by crude oil (59%), natural gas (24%) and biomass wastes (17%). The consumption of primary energy is assessed at 8.8 Mtoe, covered prevalently by fuel products at 49% and natural gas at 38% (Figure 2). A great part of the primary energy (6.20 Mtoe in 2001) is consumed in the production of about 12 billion kWh of electricity chiefly used in the industrial sector and households air-conditioning and lighting (Figure 3). Gas and town gas are the other form of energy which is used in the domestic sector in the heating of water. There are no accurate estimates on the number of installed gas and town gas water heaters in the whole country but studies conducted by the National institute of staticin the early 2005s indicated a range between 500,000 and 600,000 [18]. Unelectrified Tunisian rural households consume about 7 kg of wood fuel/day and 2.25 l of kerosene daily, of which 25% is used for water heating. The increase of the price same us the demand in primary energy has directly affected the economic growth of the country [19]. Although in 2012, the country has made little progress conferred by the peaceful Tunisian revolution which seems to be a new chance to speed up reforms and improve governance, competitiveness and respect for human rights. The Tunisian revolution hopes for recovery are good thanks to sound macroeconomic policy. In fact, during the six months of 2012 the economic growth increased to reach 4.8%.

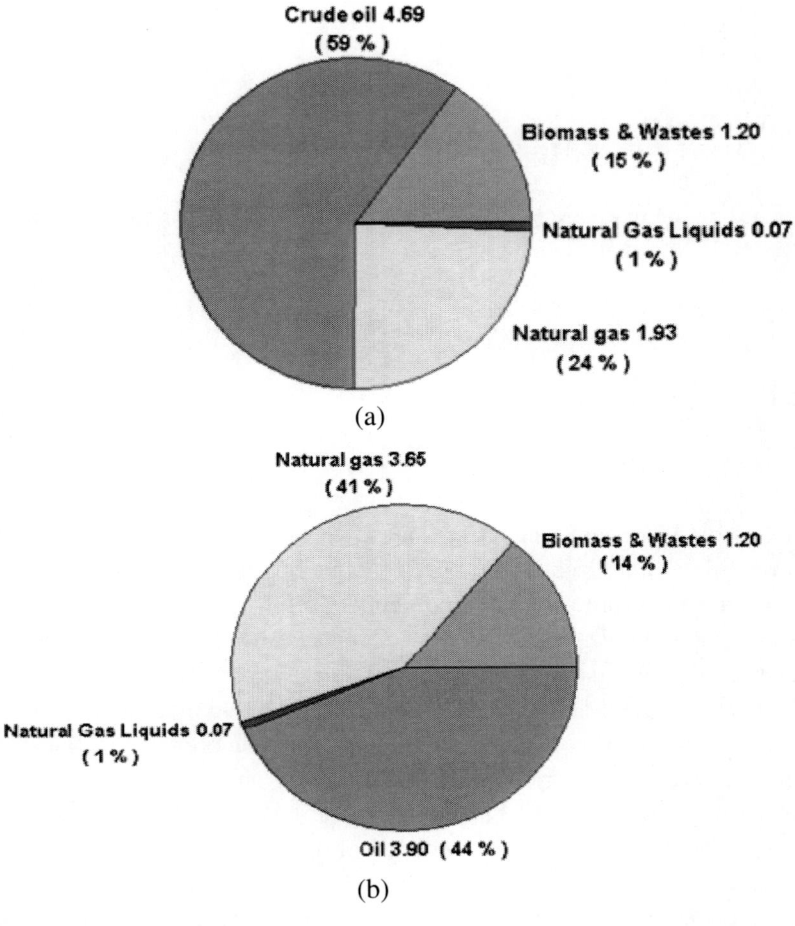

Figure 2. Diagram of the Tunisian production (a) and consumption (b) (in Mtoe, %, in 2007).

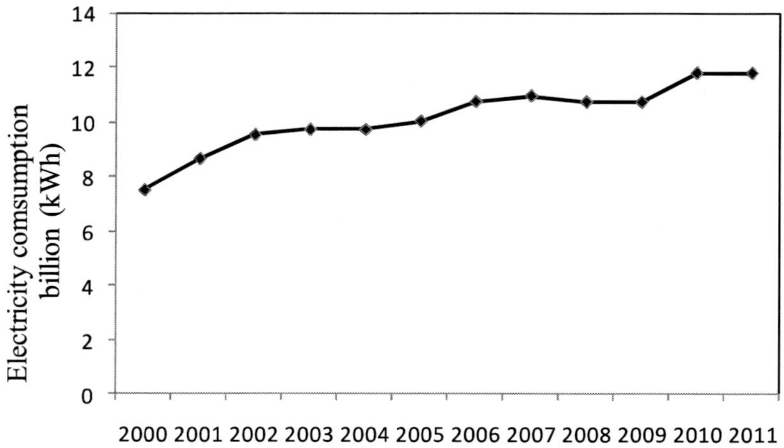

Figure 3. Total electric consumption in Tunisia (2000-2011).

2.2. Energy Strategy

Over the last ten years, the national choices in energy (rational use of energy, development of natural gas consumption) and development (emphasis placed on low-energy intensive industries and a service-focused economy) have led to the decoupling of air pollutant emissions (GHG emissions), according to Kyoto protocol, and economic growth. Consequently, Tunisian policy makers have begun acknowledging the need to resort to cleaner and renewable energy sources, particularly solar energy, hydropower and Wind. Furthermore, gas prices will be supported to promote more general use of gas in all sectors and throughout the country. The support to natural gas has a direct impact on electricity prices since electricity in Tunisia is essentially supplied by gas-powered plants. The contribution of the renewable energy (RE) technologies in Tunisia accounts for 47 ktoe and represents 0.6% of the primary energy balance for 2010 (Table 1) [18, 19]. According to the strategic study on RE the potential achievable by 2010 could represent 310 MW in wind, 28 MW in biogas and 214 000 m^2 in installed DSWH systems. More recently, the government has decided to upscale developments on the DSWH market to 620 000 m^2 by 2010 [20]. The 11th Economic Development Plan in Tunisia targets 640 MToe in energy savings by 2010 through ambitious objectives to upscale the policy on Rational Use of Energy (RUE) in all sectors and in "technological" areas, such as cogeneration, building heat insulation, energy certification of household appliances, more efficient lighting. Recently, Tunisia has strongly reinforced the regulatory framework governing energy savings with the enforcement of Law 2004-72 to consolidate promotional texts, to clarify the energy savings concept, to increase the responsibilities of the National Energy Savings Agency) and to increase financial support to RUE initiatives. Decree n°2005-2234 has further enlarged the scope by increasing the subsidies for energy savings initiatives from 5% to 20%, and by adding a 20% subsidy for the purchase of solar water heaters. Total financial resources to implement the savings plan have been estimated at $2.5 billion, including $175 million from the National Fund, $530 million from the public sector, $1,660 million from private sector funds, and $24 million from international cooperation, all to be spent by 2016 on 40 renewable energy projects [20]. In 2005, the ANME, the Société Tunisienne de l'Electricité et de Gaz (STEG) and the Italian Ministry for the Environment provides an example of solar thermal market development program called PROSOL. PROSOL program is created in order to boost the solar water heating market through an innovative mechanism combining investment subsidies and interests rebate, with loans from the banking sector. This helps offset the high initial cost of the systems, providing an acceptable payback period to various end users to stimulate the market. The market has undergone major recovery with PROSOL and has attracted new industrial operators and installer. According this project, Tunisian DSWH systems are projected to see steady growth in the upcoming decades, alongside other renewable energy projects for Tunisia [19, 20]. A 740,000-square-meter water heater park was installed in 2011, and a further 1,500,000 square meters will be developed by 2020, plus 2,500,000 square meters by 2030.

Table 1. Contribution of RE in the conventional primary energy balance of Tunisia

	Primary energy consumption (1000 toe)	Share (%)
Oil products	4 127	48.7%
Natural Gas	3 184	37.6%
Renewable Energies	47	0.6%
Biomass	1 112	13.1%
TOTAL	8 470	100%

3. DSWH Systems in Tunisia

All the commercialized DSWH systems in Tunisia are imported from Europe, America and Asia. The most popular one is the glazed flat-plate collector (FPC) DSWHs (Figure 4) [7, 8] consists of: (i) a painted black flat-plate copper used as absorber in which is integrated a cooper tubes used as heat exchanger, (ii) the absorber plate is mounted in an adequate casing with a clear covering and insulation to protect the absorber plate from losses of heat energy, (iii) an insulated corrosion resistant steel hot water storage tank. The hot water storage tank height and diameter are 1680 mm and 580 mm respectively, with 300 L storage capacity and an operating pressure of 3 bars. The storage tank was fitted with two immersion heaters of 9.0 kW.Thehot water storage tank is located above the collector, and water will circulate by natural convection "thermosiphon" whenever solar energy in the collector adds energy to the water in the collector leg and thus establishes a density gradient. Occasionally the domestic water heating system utilizes a pump to circulate water from the insulated storage tank to the solar collector and back to the tank. Recently a new type of DSWH system based on evacuated tube solar collector (ETC) is commercialized in the Tunisian domestic/tertiaire sector. It consists of a row of transparent parallel 24 heat pipe evacuated tubes, with a vacuum level of 10-5 mbar, integrated into hot water storage tank (Figure 5). Each tube contains a glass outer tube and metal absorber tube attached to a fin. The evacuated tube collector produces higher temperature water than flat-plate collector systems.

Table 2. FPC parameters

Parameters	**Value**	**unit**
Collector absorber area	4	m^2
Number in series	2	-
Test flow rate	100	$Kg. h^{-1}.m^{-2}$
Fluid specific heat	4.184	$kJ.kg^{-1}.k^{-1}$
Collector slope	45	Degrees
Absorber plate emittance	0.70	-
Absorbance	0.8	-
Heat loss coefficient U_L	$W.m^{-2}.K^{-1}$	2.3

In Table 2, 3 and 4 is presented the parameters of FPC, ETC and the hot water tank respectively. Installations No. 1 and No. 2 can use both beam and diffuse solar radiation, and they do not require tracking of the sun. The maximum efficiency of a FPC DSWH system ranges from 50% to 70% with heat normally delivered between323.15 and 348.15 K. ETC DSWH system has lower thermal losses due to an internal vacuum and less dependence on solar angle due to cylindrical geometry. Therefore, ETC DSWH system can reach temperature up to 393.15 K, with a normal efficiency around 50–80%. However, the price for evacuated tube collectors is more expensive than the flat-plate collectors.

Figure 4. Flat-plate DSWH system.

Figure 5. Evacuated tube DSWH system.

Table 3. ETC parameters

Parameters	Value	Unit
Collector area	1.7	m^2
Number in parallel	2	-
Number of heat pipe tubes	30	-
Distance between tubes	10	cm
Tested flow rate	100	$Kg.h^{-1}.m^{-2}$
Fluid specific heat	4.184	$kJ.kg^{-1}.k^{-1}$
Collector slope	45	Degrees
Absorber plate emittance	0.87	-
Absorbance	0.91	-
Heat loss coefficient U_L	1.2	$W.m^{-2}.K^{-1}$

Table 4. Hot water storage cylinder parameters

Parameters	**Value**	**Unit**
User specified inlet positions	2	-
Tank volume	0.3	m^3
Tank height	1.68	m
Height of flow inlet1	0.2	m
Height of flow outlet 1	1.6	m
Fluid specific heat	4.19	$kJ.kg^{-1}.K^{-1}$
Fluid density	10^3	$kg.m^{-3}$
Tank loss coefficient	1.6	$W.m^{-2}\ K^{-1}$
Boiling temperature	373.15	K
Height of 1st auxiliary heater	1.5	m
Height of 1st thermostat	1.5	m
Set point temperature for element1	333.15	K
Dead band for heating element	288.15	K
Maximum heating rate of element	9	kW

4. CASE STUDY

To highlight the benefits of using DSWHs in Tunisia, a case study was considered for a typical Tunisian household with 4-5 occupants. The selected region for the investigation is Borj CEDRIA (Tunis), situated in the north of Tunisia (36° 379 N to 42° 029 N) (Figure 6). The study is achieved for the most commercialized FPC DSWHs (Installation No. 1) and ETC DSWHs (Installation No. 2) in Tunisia. Studies [7, 8] illustrated that for a typical Tunisian family composed of 4-5 peoples the hot water consumption was estimated about 265 l/day.

The study of the energetic potential given by the use of DSWHs a TRNSYS simulation model is achieved with Typical Meteorological Year (TMY) for Borj cedria data, Tunis, Tunisia. In Table 5 is presented the parameters of the studied case. The results of the TRNSYS model are used to evaluate the energy collected, the energy extracted and delivered to the user, heat loss, auxiliary energy and solar fraction relative to the two installations (No. 1 and No. 2).The results of the TRNSYS model are also used to evaluate the savings, financial viability, payback times and the environmental aspects for the two installations (No. 1 and No. 2).To achieve this simulation the TRNSYS model need various inputs The methodology in this work consists in: (i) the determination of the experimental inputs of the TRNSYS simulation model of the two installations (No. 1 and No. 2) characteristics like the dimensions of all components, the efficiency, storage tank and energy losses) by means of a primary experimental test, (ii) the simulation of the performances of the installations No. 1 and No. 2 during selected days of July 2012 by using TRNSYS model, (iii) the verification that the elaborated TRNSYS model presents suitable results by comparing the simulated and the experimental results and (iv) once the validation is achieved we presume that the elaborated TRNSYS model could serves as a valid simulation tools for evaluating the annual performances of the two installations (No. 1 and No. 2) by introduction the meteorological year for Borj cedria, Tunis, Tunisia. The annual performances of the two installations (No. 1 and No. 2) are then compared to conventional water heating technologies (electric and gas/town gas heater) according to Tunisian scenario.

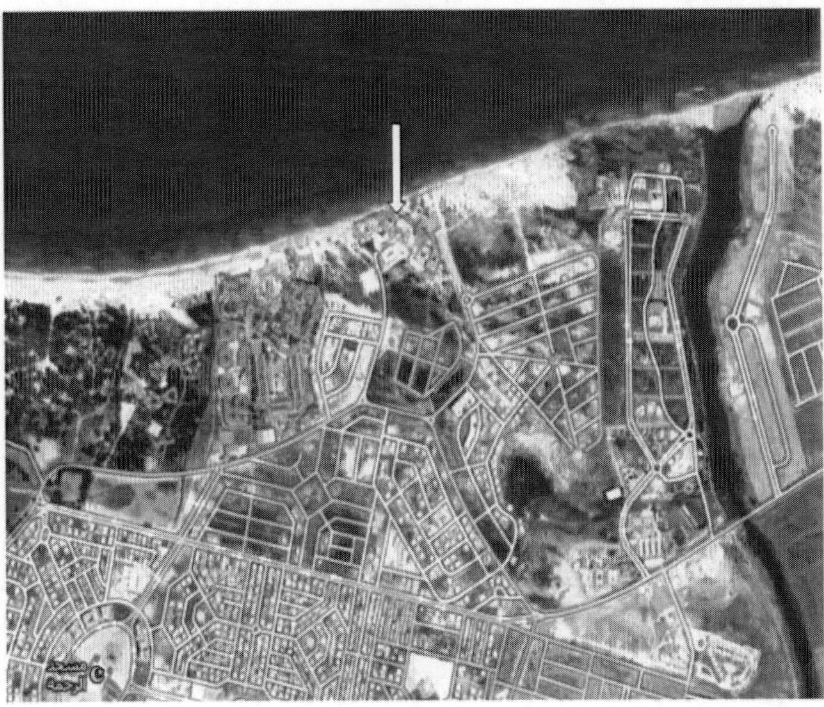

Figure 6. Localization of the study area.

Table 5. Parametres of the studied case

Parametres	Value
Average number of peaple / house	4-5
Occupancy rate (%)	90
Daily hot water usage estimation (L/day)	265
Hot water temperature (K)	318.15
Operating days per week	7
Solar water heater types	FPC and ETC
Conventinal fuel type	Electricity, gas, tawn/gas
Electricity rate ($)	0.026
Inflation rate (%)	3
Project life (years)	25
GHG emission factor for natural gas (tCO_2/MWh)	0.780

5. Experimental Apparatus and Protocol

A schematic of the proposed framework is depicted in Figure 7. The framework is performed in order to determine the TRNSYS program inputs (i.e., solar collector efficiency and storage cylinder heat loss coefficient) of the two installations in the target area. The experimental investigation is based on (I/O) test method developed as a draft of test standard (EN 12975, ISO 9806:2012) [7]. Immersed Pt100 sensors were placed at the midpoint of the hot water cylinder to measure the hot water temperature, TS. The inlet, Tin and outlet temperature, Tout, of the FPC and ETC are measured by using Pt100 sensors placed at the inlet and the outlet of the two solar collectors. Another Pt100 sensor was placed out of the solar collector to measure the ambient air temperature. The incident solar radiation, G, was measured with a Kipp and Zonen pyranometre installed such that its aperture is leveled with the aperture of the collector without casting shadow on the collector. All of these parameters were measured by a multi-channel digital data acquisition data at an interval of 5 s. The mainly results of the experimental test are intercept efficiency, the first order efficiency coefficient (c_1) and the second order efficiency coefficient (c_2). The heat loss coefficient (U_c) of the hot water tank storage is determined in an independent test by measuring the hot water cylinder temperature decrease while the hot water cylinder is left to cool down during about 24 h. Additional inputs that may be required by some calculation methods include the position (horizontal or vertical), insulation levels and controls. The heat loss coefficient (Uc) of the hot water storage cylinder is determined by an independent test. It consists in: (i) heating the water inside the stainless steel storage tank ($V = 0.3m^3$) to the value of 317 K (Ti), then the immersion heaters were set to turn-off, (ii) measuring the temperature decrease of the hot water in the stainless steel storage tank while the hot water is left to cool down during $\Delta t = 24$ h (Tf). U_C is calculated as:

$$U_C = \frac{C_p}{V.\Delta t} \ln \frac{T_i - T_{ext}}{T_f - T_{ext}} \qquad (1)$$

Uncertainty analysis is needed to prove the accuracy of the experiments. In this study, errors came from the sensitiveness of equipment and measurements explained previously. First; errors due to measurement of temperature are: (i) sensitiveness of data acquisition system, about ±0.1% and (ii) measurement error is ±0.2%. The sensitiveness was obtained from a catalog of the instruments. Second, errors came from the measurement of the flow rate: (i) the sensitiveness of the flow meter is about ±0.1% and (ii) errors due to measurement are about ±0.1%. In total, errors of measurement of the flow rate are about ±0.2%. The total uncertainties associated with the calculated values were found as follows: (i) ±2% for solar collector's instantaneous thermal efficiency and (ii) the value of the temperature changes in the storage tank and in the inlet and outlet of the solar collector.

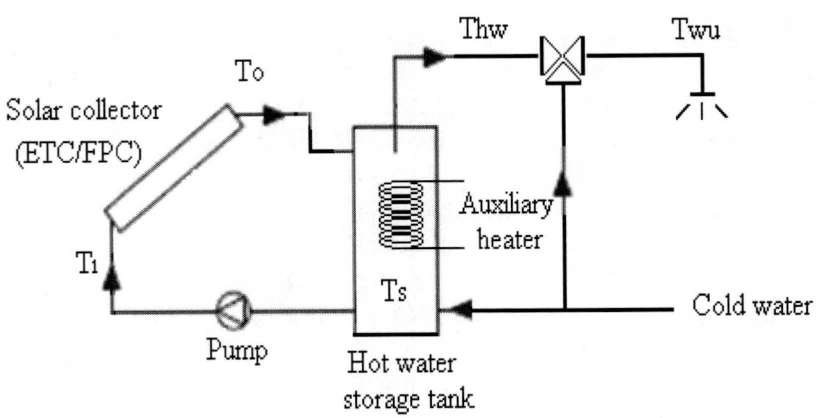

Figure 7. Schematic of the two installations (No. 1 and No. 2).

6. TRNSYS SIMULATION MODEL

The main component of the TRNSYS model is the solar collector which is either a flat-plate collector (Type 1) or evacuated tube collector (Type 71). Additional components to the model include: Type 31 pipe duct, Type 4c hot water cylinder with 2 inlets and 2 outlet, Type 2b differential temperature controller, Type 3b variable speed pump, Type 14 forcing functions, Type 65 online plotter and Type 25b simulation summary. Type 14b forcing functions were used several times in the model to input ambient air temperature and mains water supply temperature (Type 14e), wind speed (Type 14g), immersion heater control signals and in-plane solar radiation (Type 14h). Weather data of the target area includes the ambient temperature and radiation data. For a given hot water usage pattern, discrete sizes of collector area and corresponding storage tank capacity are considered based on existing commercially available systems. The system considered for simulation is a forced flow DSWH systems with FPC and ETC. The simulation is done on an hourly basis for a period of one year using monthly average hourly weather data and hourly hot water requirement. The weather data includes hourly global solar radiation; diffuse solar radiation and ambient temperatures. TRNSYS is employing the standard second-order collector performance equation to model the collector, given by:

$$\eta = \eta_0 - c_1 \frac{T_m - T_{ext}}{G} - c_2 (\frac{T_m - T_{ext}}{G})^2 \qquad (2)$$

where $\eta_0 = c_0 K_\theta$ is the intercept efficiency and c_1 and c_2 are respectively the first order efficiency coefficient and the second order efficiency coefficient. K_θ is the Incidence Angle Modified (IAM). The output of the simulation is hourly auxiliary heating required. For a given collector area and storage area, the simulation using TRNSYS provides the total annual extracted energy, the auxiliary heating requirement and the solar fraction for a specific hot water usage pattern. The technical potential for DSWHs and the energy savings depends on the auxiliary heating requirement. Table 6 show TRNSYS model inputs parameters for the installations No. 1 and No. 2.

Table 6. ETC and FPC TRNSYS input data

Parameters	FPC	ETC	Unit
Tested flow rate	80	80	$Kg.h^{-1}.m^{-2}$
Intercept efficiency, η_0	0.71	0.74	%
First order efficiency coefficient, a_1	14.11	1.5	$kJ.kg^{-1}.m^{-2}.k^{-1}$
Second order efficiency coefficient, a_2	0.054	0.002	$kJ.kg^{-1}.m^{-2}.k^{-2}$
Hot water tank heat loss coefficient (U_c)	3	1.8	$W.m^{-2}\ K^{-1}$
Collector slope	45	45	Degrees

7. Thermal Performances and Economic Analysis of DSWHs

Once the TRNSYS simulation is validated by experimental measurements we achieve the simulation along the whole year of 2012 to estimate the energy needs of a typical Tunisian house (or apartment) under different environment conditions (Sunny, and cloudy and rainy conditions). Accordingly, the TRNSYS simulation is used for evaluating the annual performances of the two installations by introduction the Typical Meteorological Year (TMY) for Borj cedria data, Tunis, Tunisia.

7.1. Thermal Performances

Through TRNSYS simulation model we evaluated the monthly/annual performances of the two installations (No. 1 and No. 2). In Table 7 we presented the monthly/annual solar insolation, energy extracted, energy lost, auxiliary electric energy, thermal efficiencies and solar fraction for both of installations (No. 1 and No. 2). Figure 8 illustrates the monthly/annual energy flows for both of installations (No. 1 and No. 2). It includes the total radiation incident on the collector (Q_I), the useful energy supplied from the collectors (Q_C), the extracted energy (Q_{Ext}), the auxiliary energy demand (Q_{Aux}), the heat losses from the storage tank (Q_{lost}) and the solar fraction. We perceive from figure that the useful energy supplied from the collectors (Q_C) is maximized in the month of July, about 133. kWh/m^2 and 139.76 kWh/m^2 for the installations No. 1 and No. 2, respectively. It can be also seen from Figure 8 that during the month of February there is a reduction in the incident solar radiation, 455.03

kWh/m^2, and consequently the useful energy collected, about 89.7 kWh/m^2 and 97.7 kWh/m^2 for the installations No. 1 and No. 2, respectively. The annual value of the useful energy supplied by solar energy (QC) is equal to 1378.62 kWh/m^2 and 1497.76 kWh/m^2 for the installations No. 1 and No. 2, respectively. Figure 8 shows also that the auxiliary electric energy consumed in the installation No. 1 and No. 2 are about 404.88 kWh/m^2 and 291.06 kWh/m^2 respectively. They represent almost 29.3 and 19.4% of the energy collected by the installations No. 1 and No. 2. However we mention that the auxiliary electric energy consumed in the installation No. 2 is lesser than that consumed by the installation No. 1. In Figure 11 is also represented the monthly energy extracted during the whole year of 2012 for the two installations given by the relation:

$$Q_{Ext} = Q_{Aux} + [Q_C - Q_{lost}] \quad (3)$$

where Q_{lost} is the annual energy lost from the storage tank and pipes, Q_C is the annual energy collected from each the solar collector and Q_{Aux} is the annual auxiliary energy. We notes that the energy extracted increase during the cold months of the year (November to March). The maximum rate of the extracted energy is reached in January, with a value about 155.8 kWh/m^2 and 158 kWh/m^2 for the installations No. 1 and No. 2, respectively. During the hot months of the year the rates of the extracted energy decrease. We establish that there is a decrease of hot water demand during the summer months compared to cold months. Throughout the year a rate of 1555.4 kWh/m^2 and 1618.8 kWh/m^2 of heat energy were extracted from the installations No. 1 and No. 2 and delivered to the users. From the curve of the energy lost from storage tank (Q_{lost}) it can be seen that during summer months the energy lost from storage to surroundings is maximized. This is due to the fact that at these months the temperature in the storage tank is higher and consequently more energy is lost. Table 7 shows that the annual energy losses represent almost 14.6% of the energy extracted from the installation No. 1 and 10.5% of the installation No. 2. In Figure 8 is represented the monthly solar fraction variation for the two installations [21, 22].

$$f = \frac{Q_{Ext} - Q_{Aux}}{Q_{Ext}} \quad (4)$$

where, Q_{Ext} is the total energy extracted from the system to support the water heating requirements and Q_{Aux} is the total auxiliary energy supplied to the system to support the portion of the total load that is not provide by the solar energy. We note that the solar fraction of the installation No. 1 ranged between 46% and 89% in January and July respectively while the solar fraction for the installation No. 2 ranged between 59% and 100% in January and July respectively. The installations No. 1 and No. 2 had annual average solar fraction of 68% and 84% respectively. In Table 8 we present the efficiencies changes vs months of 2012. We notice that the annual efficiencies of the two installations are about 67% (No. 1) and 76% (No. 2) respectively.

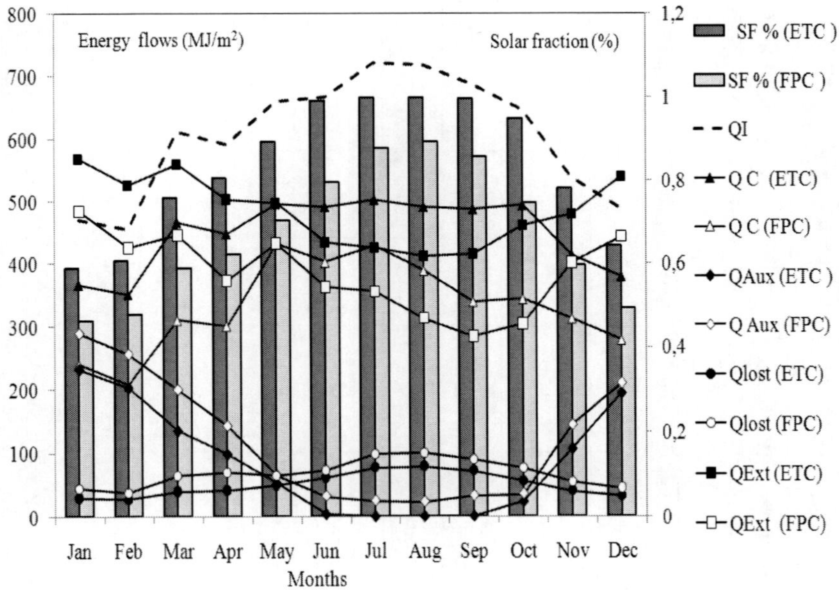

Figure 8. Monthly and yearly energy flows variation for the installations No. 1 and No. 2.

Table 7. Monthly and annual energy collected, auxiliary energy need and solar fraction for the of the two installations (No. 1 and No. 2) predicted by TRNSYS program

Month	Solar insulation (kWh/m^2.month)	Energy collected (kWh/m^2.month)		Auxiliary energy (kWh/m^2.month)		Energy lost (kWh /m^2.month)		Energy extracted (kWh m^2.month)		Solar fraction (%)	
		No.1	No.2	No.1	No.2	No.1	No.2	No.1	No.2	No.1	No.2
Jan	470,60	87,73	101,93	80,31	64,45	12,28	8,40	155,76	157,98	0,46	0,59
Feb	455,03	89,66	97,66	71,15	56,38	10,53	7,84	150,28	146,21	0,47	0,60
Mar	611,30	113,76	129,53	55,59	37,42	18,09	11,15	151,26	155,79	0,59	0,75
Apr	591,60	117,43	124,44	39,59	27,20	19,5	11,68	137,53	139,96	0,62	0,80
May	660,62	123,86	137,94	18,10	14,44	18,11	13,99	123,85	138,39	0,70	0,89
Jun	667,39	123,56	136,63	9,06	1,04	20,33	17,13	112,3	120,55	0,79	0,99
Jul	721,13	133,3	139,76	7,01	0	27,28	21,49	113,03	118,26	0,87	1
Aug	717,38	126,04	136,55	6,53	0	27,84	21,95	104,74	114,60	0,89	1
Sep	687,37	129,09	135,43	9,20	0,23	24,93	20,20	113,35	115,44	0,85	0,99
Oct	647,86	128,26	137,25	9,96	6,44	21,26	15,63	116,96	128,06	0,75	0,95
Nov	539,45	110,36	115,07	39,96	29,54	15,34	11,33	134,99	133,27	0,60	0,78
Dec	489,39	95,52	105,5	58,36	53,88	12,59	9,20	141,29	150,178	0,49	0,64
Annual total	7259,19	1378,62	1497,76	404,88	291,06	228,12	170,07	1555,38	1618,75		
Annual average	604,93	114,88	124,81	33,73	24,25	19,00	14,17	129,61	134,89	0,68	0,84

Table 8. The predicted efficiencies of the two installations (No. 1 and No. 2) calculated by TRNSYS program

Month	Solar insulation (kWh/m^2. month)	No. 1	No. 2
Jan	470,60	0,67	0,78
Feb	455,03	0,7	0,77
Mar	611,30	0,66	0,76
Apr	591,60	0,71	0,75
May	660,62	0,67	0,75
Jun	667,39	0,66	0,74
Jul	721,13	0,66	0,7
Aug	717,38	0,63	0,68
Sep	687,37	0,67	0,71
Oct	647,86	0,71	0,76
Nov	539,45	0,73	0,77
Dec	489,39	0,7	0,78
Annual total	7259,19		
Annual average	604,93	0,67	0,76

7.2. Economic Analysis

The economic analysis (DSWH system cost, energy price and payback period in comparison with the expected service life of the installation) are the other major concern of the study [23]. It is performed by comparing the cumulative energy invested, CE, with the energy saved by the solar system throughout its service life. The economic scenario used in this project is that all the cost of the solar system is paid from the beginning (i.e., no credit payments are assumed). The thermal performance degradation of the system is assumed to be 2% per year, the period of economic analysis is taken as 20 years (average life of locally produced systems), whereas all the other percentage figures (inflation rates and market discount rate) are mean values of the previous decade (Statistical abstracts, 2012). Electricity at a price of 0.1508 $ per kWh and gas at a price of 0.2482 $ per m^3 are assumed to be used for auxiliary.

The cumulative energy invested (CE) in the DSWH system's lifecycle is the sum of the energy required for the fuel cycle (EFC) and the energy requirements during the construction (CE), transportation, operation and maintenance (ETOM), and decommissioning, refurbishment and recycling phases (EDRR).

The energy for fuel cycle (EFC) is obtained by considering the energy flows of each process in their lifecycle. A typical fossil fuel lifecycle includes exploration, production and delivery of the resources.

To determine the energy requirement during the construction (CE), the total energy obtained from electricity consumption must be transformed to primary energy conversion factor (PEF). The mean primary conversion factor is assumed to be 2.7 for the electric domestic use [24] and 1.1 for fuel use. The electrical energy requirement is considered during the phases of construction and decommissioning.

The requirement for transportation, operation and maintenance (ETOM) energy is covered by the DSWH systems own production. Material and component transportation to final destination is an energy intensive process as in most cases involves the use of fossil fuels. Also, transportation is one of the sectors with the largest growth in energy use [25]. The transportation costs include those to and from the nearest available port to the location of interest in Tunisia. EDRR is assumed to be equal to the energy used in the construction phase. It is considered that the energy cost of dismantling the DSWH systems is equal to the energy cost of solar field construction and equipment assembly.

There are many uncertainties in the estimation of the cumulative energy invested (CE) in the DSWH system's lifecycle (Adrene et al. [26]). The majority of the components of the studied DSWH system's (pumps, expansion vessels, collectors, etc.) were imported from manufacturers in various countries, resulting in additional uncertainty over the CE calculations. The approach in this paper was to prepare an estimation of the CE based on the data from the previously reviewed references [22, 23, 24, 25, 26] (Table 9).

The energy payback (EP) indicates the amount of years that a system must operate in order to produce the same amount of energy than was required for its construction and operation. The energy payback (EP) for the two installations (No. 1 and No. 2) was calculated on the base of the number of years needed by each solar installation to save as much energy as its cumulative energy invested (CE). The energy payback (EP) in years is calculated using Eq. (5) [26]:

$$EP = \frac{\mathrm{CE}}{AES} \tag{5}$$

The annual energy savings (AES) was calculated considering the efficiency of the auxiliary heating system to which the DSWH system is substituting, and applying PEF depending on the electric domestic use fuel used. The AES was calculated by using the formula below [26]:

$$AES = \frac{Q_{Ext} \cdot PEF_{Auxiliaryheating}}{Efficiency_{Auxiliary\ heating}} - \frac{Elec.Use.Pump}{PEF_{Electr}} \quad (6)$$

The energy payback calculation, the solar energy output and associated energy savings have been considered constant for every year of the installation's service life. Results of the calculation for each installation are presented in Table 9. It can be observed that energy payback periods based on the predicted performance of the installations vary considerably depending of the type of installation and substituted conventional water heating systems. For such a typical house, the annual savings in electrical energy and payback period relatively to the installation No. 1, were found 1316 kWh/year and 8 years based on electric water heater, or 306 m3gas/town gas saving and 6 years payback period based on gas water heater, respectively. For the installation No. 2 the annual electricity saving and payback period were found 1459 kWh/year and 10 years based on electric water heater, or 410 m3gas/town gas saving and 7.5 years payback period based on gas water heater, respectively. The relatively lengthy payback period is due to the expensive shipment/transportation cost of the DSWHs. These costs are expected to go down with the future growth in the solar product demands. Nevertheless, the findings suggest that the installation No. 2 may not be as attractive as the installation No. 1 for low temperature applications, since the economical payback of the latter is around 2 years shorter. As can be seen the solar system gives much lower specific energy cost than the conventional system for both types of auxiliary energy considered. The life cycle savings represent the money that the owner will save by installing the solar system (Installations No. 1 and No. 2) instead of buying electricity/gas/town gas to satisfy his hot water needs and is about 3969 $ (Installation No. 1) and 4400.34$ (Installation No. 2) for electricity backup and is about 1517.76 $ (Installation No. 1) and 2035.24 $ (Installation No. 2) for gas/town gas backup.

The energy return of energy invested (ER) provides more accurate information of the life cycle energy performance of the systems, and can be directly compared with ER values for other renewable technologies [27]. The ER of a DSWH system is calculated as the service life (SL) divided by the energy payback (Eq. 7).

$$ER = \frac{SL}{EP} \tag{7}$$

The comparison of the ER result is compared with photovoltaic renewable energy shows that for a typical on-site PV installation the CE are about 1700kWh per square meter [27, 28]. Its yearly energy savings in primary energy terms and the energy payback would be 304 kWh and 6 years. Applying Eq. (7) to these values, assuming a service life of 20 years for the PV systems, the ER would be equal to 3.3. While the ER of DSWH systems based on expected systems performances is in all cases greater than the ER for PV systems, typically varying between 5 and 15. These results serve as a confirmation of the potential of DSWHs to provide large life cycle energy savings [23, 24, 25, 26, 28].

Table 9. Calculation of the cumulative energy invested (CE)

Installation	Pump	Storage tank	Collectors	Heat ex-changer	Total system components	Total installation*
No. 1	0	1000	3160	1050	5410	6492
No. 2	120	4000	6888	1400	13128	17754

*20% margin has been added to the total calculated CE from the inventory analysis to account for transport, maintenance and disposal, as discussed in a sensitivity analysis by Ardente et al. [26].

8. Generalized Analysis to All Tunisia

According to ANME the calculated consumption for an average 9 kW residential electric water heater is 2555 kWh/year. The cost of solar heated water is estimated to \$0.24/L, which is less than electrically heated water (\$0.27/L), but more than fuel heated water (\$0.20/L). Nowadays there is about 740,000-square-meter collector area of DSWHs is installed in Tunisia by the year 2011 (about 75% flat-plate solar collector DSWHs and about 25%

evacuated tubes solar collector DSWHs). The main consumer of hot water is the residential sector with 108,000 m^3/day, followed by hotels consuming 1140 m^3/day, health establishments consuming 478 m^3/day, and educational institutions with 220 m^3/day. The results of investigating illustrate that there is a considerable gain in saving energy in addition of the profitable investment for both household owners and the government as demonstrated previously (Table 10). Indeed the installations of DSWHs permit the savings of about 500 million kWh of electricity per year which represents about 20% of the total electric energy consumption (respectively about 365.2 million kWh/year and 135 kWh/year for the installations No. 1 and No. 2). If gas heaters are in use, the equivalent volumes of gas/town gas consumed are 84.9 million m^3 and 37.9 million m^3. It would also reduce the energy by $30 million over 10 years. From an environmental point of view the net annual GHG emission per house is reduced by 27800 tCO2 [30, 31, 32]. The rate of saved energy and the net annual GHG emission per house may become more important when we considered that, according to ANME, about 1,500.000 square meters water heater will be installed and exploited by 2020, which represent about 25% of total households implanted in Tunisia and further 2,500,000 square meters will be installed by 2030, which represent about 84% of total households.

Table. 10. Life cycle savings and payback periods of the two installations (No. 1 and No. 2) according to the electric and Gas energy

	FPC DSWH system	ETC DSWH system
System cost	940$	1100$
Installation cost	20$	20$
Upholding cost	40$	60$
Electricity saving	1316 kWh/year	1459 kWh/year
Life cycle savings based on electricity saving	3969 $	4400.34 $
Gas saving	306 m^3	410 m^3
Life cycle savings based on gas saving	1517.76 $	2035.24 $
Payback period	8 years (based on electric water heater)	10 years(based on electric water heater)
	6 years (based on gas water heater)	7.5 years (based on gas water heater)

SUMMARY AND CONCLUSION

This paper investigates the potential of DSWHs in the reduction of electrical energy and gas/natural gas use for water heating and environmental benefits in Tunisia by making a comparative evaluation of water heating practices in the domestic sector. A scenario through a case study in Borj cedria, Tunis, Tunisia (36° 379 N to 42° 029 N), representing mild and hot climates was achieved by means of TRNSYS simulation program for the two mostly commercialized DSWHs installations (DSWH system based on flat-plate solar collector, No. 1, and DSWH system based on evacuated tubes solar collector, No. 2). The main results of the simulation of the two installations behavior's presume that throughout the year a rate of 1555.4 kWh/m^2 and 1618.8kWh/m^2 of heat energy may extracted from the installations No. 1 and No. 2 and delivered to the users. The TRNSYS simulation presume also that annual energy losses represent almost 14.6% of the energy extracted from the installation No. 1 and 10.5% of the installation No. 2 and the auxiliary electric energy consumed in the installation No. 1 and No. 2 were about 404.88 kWh/m^2 and 291.06 kWh/m^2 respectively. However we mention that the auxiliary electric energy consumed in the installation No. 2 is lesser than that consumed by the installation No. 1. Additional major benefits of installing DSWHs were assessed. One is the cost saving generated by replacing conventional energies, and the other is avoiding the costs associated with reducing GHGs and pollutant emissions. For such a Tunisian typical house, the annual savings in electrical energy and payback period relatively to the installation No. 1, were found 1316 kWh/year and 8 years based on electric water heater, or 306 m3gas/town gas saving and 6 years payback period based on gas water heater, respectively. For the installation No. 2 the annual electricity saving and payback period were found 1459 kWh/year and 10 years based on electric water heater, or 410 m3gas/town gas saving and 7.5 years payback period based on gas water heater, respectively. The life cycle savings instead of buying electricity/gas/town gas to satisfy his hot water needs and is about 3969 $ (Installation No. 1) and 4400.34 $ (Installation No.2) for electricity backup and is about 1517.76 $ (Installation No.1) and 2035.24 $ (Installation No. 2) for gas/town gas backup. From an environment point of view the GHGs emissions can be reduced by approximately 150,000 tons yearly. Regarding the analysis presented in this paper it can be concluded that solar energy systems are efficient, cost effective and friendlier to the environment. The reduction of greenhouse gasses pollution is the main advantage of utilizing solar energy. Therefore, solar energy systems should be employed whenever possible in order to achieve a sustainable future.

References

[1] Amous S. Energy Efficiency and Renewable Energies Tunisia. Mediterranean and National Strategies for Sustainable Development.plan Bleu; 2007. [1] OECD/IEA. Country file.TUNISIA; 2010.

[2] Ardente F, Beccali G, Cellura M, Brano VL. Life cycle assessment of a solar thermal collector. *Renewable Energy* 2005;30 :1031–1054.

[3] Amous S. Energy Efficiency and Renewable Energies Tunisia. Mediterranean and National Strategies for Sustainable Development. *Plan Bleu,* 2007.

[4] Ardente F, Beccali G, Cellura M, Lo Brano V. Life cycle assessment of a solar thermal collector. *Renewable Energy* 2005;30:1031–54.

[5] Battisti R, Corrado A. Environmental assessment of solar thermal collectors with integrated water storage. *Journal of Cleaner Production* 2005; 13: 1295–300.

[6] Belloumi M. Energy consumption and GDP in Tunisia: Cointegration and causality analysis. *Energy Polic*y 2009;37: 2745–2753.

[7] Chebbi HE, Olarreaga M, Zitouna H. Trade Openness And CO_2 Emissions In Tunisia. *Middle East Development Journal* 2011; 3: 29-53.

[8] Crawford RH, Treloar GJ, Llozor B.D, Love PED. Comparative greenhouse emissions analysis of domestic solar hot water systems, *Building Research and Information* 2003;31: 34–47.

[9] EN ISO 9806: 2012/ EN ISO DIS 9806:2012. Solar Energy-Solar thermal collectors-Test methods.

[10] Hassairi M. The greenhouses gases generation in Tunisia: analysis and abatement. Proceedings of the World RenewableEnergy Congress Brighton, England 2000 : 2591–2595.

[11] Hazami M, Kooli S, Lazâar M, Farhat A, Belghith A. Energetic and exergetic performances of an economical and available integrated solar storage collector based on concrete matrix. *Energy Conversion and Management* 2010;51: 1210–1218.

[12] Hernandez P, Kenny P. Net energy analysis of domestic solar water heating installations in operation, *Renewable and Sustainable Energy Reviews* 2012;16 :170– 177.

[13] Kalogirou S. Environmental benefits of domestic solar energy systems. *Energy Conversion and Management* 2004; 45: 3075–92.

[14] Kalogirou S. Thermal performance, economic and environmental life cycle analysis of thermosiphon solar water heaters. *Solar Energy* 2009; 83: 39–48. [15] TRNSYS. TRNSYS, transient systems simulation program; 2010. http://sel.me.wisc.edu/trnsys/.

[15] Khemiri A, Hassairi M. Development of energy efficiency improvement in the Tunisian hotel sector: a case study. *Renewable Energy* 2005; 30 : 903–911.

[16] S. Kalogirou, Thermal performance, economic and environmental life cycle analysis of thermosiphon solar water heaters, *Solar Energy* 2009;83 : 39–48.

[17] Ramana MV., Ashwin K. Least cost principles and electricity planning for Karnataka. *Energy for Sustainable Development* 2009; 13: 225–234.

[18] Ramazan S, Ugur S. The growth of income and energy consumption in six developing countries, *Energy Policy* 2007; 35: 889–898.

[19] Ramakrishnan R. An analysis of energy consumption and carbon dioxide emissions in countries of the Middle East and North Africa. *Energy,* 2005;30: 2831–2842.

[20] Raugei M, Bargigli S, Ulgiati S. Life cycle assessment and energy pay-back time of advanced photovoltaic modules: CdTe and CIS compared to poly-Si. *Energy* 2007;32:1310–8.

[21] Rey-Martinez FJ, Velasco-Gomez E, Martin-Gil J, NavasGracia LM, Hernandez Navarro S. Life cycle analysis of a thermal solar installation at a rural house in Valladolid (Spain). *Environmental Engineering Science* 2008;25: 713–723.

[22] Richards BS, Watt ME. Permanently dispelling a my th of photovoltaics via the adoption of a new net energy indicator. *Renewable and Sustainable Energy Reviews* 2007;11: 162–72.

[23] Nawaz I, Tiwari GN. Embodied energy analysis of photovoltaic (PV) system based on macro- and micro-level. *Energy Policy* 2006;34: 3144–52.

[24] Tsilingiridis G, Martinopoulos G. Thirty years of domestic solar hot water systems use in Greece – energy and environmental benefits – future perspectives. *Renewable Energy* 2010; 35: 490–497.

[25] Tsilingiridis G, Martinopoulos G, Kyriakis N. Life cycle environmental impact of a thermosyphonic domestic solar hot water system in comparison with electrical and gas water heating. *Renewable Energy* 2004; 29 : 1277–1288.

[26] TUNISIA 2010. NationalInstituteof Statistics.2010.
[27] UN-DESA REPORT, *Sustainable Energy Consumption in Africa*, 2004.
[28] Utilization of Renewable Energies in Rural Areas in Morocco, Tunisia and Jordan. European Commission, Brussels, Belgium: 1995.
[29] Wolde-Rufael Y. Electricity consumption and economic growth: a time series experience for 17 African countries. *Energy Policy* 2006;34: 1106–1114.

In: Tunisia
Editor: Eunice Wagner

ISBN: 978-1-53610-061-7
© 2016 Nova Science Publishers, Inc.

Chapter 5

PERFORMANCES PREDICTION OF A (PV/T) SOLAR COLLECTOR INTEGRATED IN INDIVIDUAL TUNISIAN HOUSEHOLDS

Majdi Hazami**, *Farah Mehdaoui, Omeima Nouicer, Nabiha Naili and Abdelhamid Farhat

Laboratoire des Procédés Thermique,
Centre de Recherches et des Technologies de l'Energie, Borj-Cedria
Hammam Lif, Tunis, Tunisia

ABSTRACT

The endeavor of this chapter is to study the potential offered by the expenditure of a PV/T solar system in Tunisian households. This investigation is performed according to two-folded approaches. Firstly, outdoor experiments were carried out during July 2014 for both passive and active mode. An exhaustive energy and exergy analysis was then performed to evaluate the instantaneous thermal and the electrical exergy outputs of the PV/T system. The results showed that the maximum instantaneous thermal and electric energy efficiency in active mode are about 50 and 15%, respectively. It was found also that the maximum thermal and electric exergy efficiencies were about 50 and 14.8%, respectively. The second approach is the evaluation of the monthly/annual performances of the PV/T solar system under typical

*Tel 71430044/71430215, Fax: 71430934. E-mail: Hazamdi321@yahoo.fr.

climate area of Tunisia by using TRNSYS program. The results showed that the active mode enhances the electric efficiency and the exergy of the PV/T solar system by 3 and 2.5% points, respectively. The results showed that the optimized PV/T solar system covert the major part of the hot water and the electric needs of Tunisian household's with an expected annual average gain of about 14.60 and 5.33%, respectively. An economic appraisal was performed.

Keywords: PV/T, energy, exergy, passive and active modes

NOMENCLATURE

A	the collector area, m²
C_p	the water specific heat, kJ/ kg·K
$\dot{E}x_{des}$	theinternal exergy losses (exergy destructions), W
$\dot{E}x_{elec}$	the electrical exergy, W
$\dot{E}x_{loss}$	theexternal exergy losses, W
$\dot{E}x_{Q,sun}$	the heat transfer exergy rate, W
$\dot{E}x_{th}$	the thermal exergy, W
F'	the PV/T solar collector efficiency factor,
F_R	the heat removal efficiency factor,
G	the total solar irradiance at collector's aperture, W/m²
Q_{th},	the useful heat gain, W
$\dot{m}$	the massflow rate in the PV/T solar collector, kg/s
I_{max}	the output current, A
$\dot{I}$	the irreversibility rate, W
K_θ	theincidence angle modifier
$\dot{S} = G.A$	the solar radiation intensity, W
T_a	the ambient temperature, K
T_{av}	the arithmetic average of the water inlet and outlet temperatures, K
T_{cell}	the cell temperature, K
T_0	the water temperature at the outlet, K
T_i	the inlet of the PV/T solar collector, K
T_{ref}	the reference temperature, K

T_{sun}	the sun's temperature, K
t_I	the test start up during the selected day, s
t_F	the test end instants during the selected day, s
U_L	the collector heat loss coefficient, W/m^2.K
U_{max}	the maximum output voltage, V

Greek Symbols

α	solar absorptance
τ	solar transmittance
$(\tau\alpha)_{PV}$	the transmittance–absorptance product of the photovoltaic PV cells,
η_{th}	thermal efficiency,%
$\bar{\eta}_{th}$	the average daily efficiency
η_{ref}	the reference electric efficiency
Ψ	the overall exergy efficiency of the PV/T solar collector,%
β	temperature coefficient

1. INTRODUCTION

1.1. Bibliography Review

Tunisia has an important potential of solar energy with an average annual solar radiation of about 26.13 MJ/m^2. This circumstance permits to Tunisia to be a lead the way in the exploitation of solar energy and management programs. Below this program several solar collectors and PV panels were installed and investigated for domestic hot water and electric production purposes. hereafter, the utilization of solar energy through solar collectors and PV panels presents a great prospect and opportunity for reducing the amount of conventional energy required with a significant potential to reduce environmental pollution arising from the use of fossil fuels. However, in PV panels, when the solar cells temperature increases, electrical voltage and efficiency decreases. Therefore, in order to achieve higher electrical efficiency, the PV panel should be regularly cooled by eliminating the heat by moving water/air through the panel. Hence a new technology of solar collector is proposed. It consists in combining PV electricity generation with thermal supply in the same hybrid photovoltaic/thermal (PV/T) solar collector. The benefit of combining these two systems lies in the reduction of the demands on physical space and the equipment cost through the use of common frames and brackets as compared to the separated PV panels and solar collectors placed side-by-side. Although the initiative of joining PV electricity generation with thermal collectors seemed promising, research on the field has been very slow compared to the significant technological advancements concerning all types of PV/T collectors.

In 2013, Dubey S and Tay AAO [1] tested two different types of hybrid PVT systems. They found that the average thermal efficiency and PV efficiency for Type (A) PV/T module are 40.7 and 11.8%, respectively, and for Type (B) are 39.4 and 11.5%, respectively. The electrical efficiency of the PV modules was also compared with and without the thermal collector, and it was found that the average PV efficiency of the PVT modules is about 0.4% higher than the normal PV module. In his work, Kalogirou.S [2] presented an analytic study which aims to the evaluation of the thermal efficiency of a conventional PV/T water solar collector. He showed that the hybrid system increases the mean annual efficiency of the PV solar system from 2.8 to 7.7% and in addition covers 49% of the hot water needs of a house. In 2015, Dupeyrat P et al., [3] investigated the efficiency of a single glazed flat plate PV/T collectors used in domestic hot water application. The thermal and electrical performances of several single glazed flat plate PV/T collectors based on water circulation were evaluated using a simple 2D thermal model under steady state conditions and different alternatives to improve the efficiency were also proposed. In order to simulate the thermal and the electric behavior of the PV/T solar collector, Haurant P et al.,[4] proposed in 2015 a simulation study based on a comparison investigation according to various evaluation criteria. The comparison was made assuming the same surface area and under the same climatic conditions. The results showed that in configuration of limited available space for solar collector area, the use of efficient PV/T collectors in the building envelop can be more advantageous than standard PV and solar thermal components. In the same context, Tomas M [5] (2014) has analyzed the performance of different concepts of solar hybrid PV/T collectors for domestic hot water application. A comparison with conventional installation of photovoltaic and thermal solar collectors with the same total collector area 100 m^2 has been done for identical load conditions.

Economic analysis based on the performance results and energy prices have also been accomplished. In their study, Sujala B et al., [6] analyzed the performance of a photovoltaic thermal system, conventional collector, and PV (photovoltaic) plate at different water storage capacities (25, 50, 75, 100, and 125 kg/m^2). Sujala Bhattarai et al., showed that the thermal efficiency of the PV/T system and the conventional collector increased sharply with increasing storage capacity. An economic study was also presented. The authors showed also that the cost payback period of PV/T system and PV plate reduced remarkably when electricity price increased from 0.049 to 0.364 US$/kWh. Besides, Mohd NAB et al., [7] presented in his work an improved design of a photovoltaic/thermal (PV/T) solar collector integrating a PV panel with a serpentine-shaped copper tube as the water heating component and a single pass air channel as the air heating component. The results indicated that when both fluids are operated independently the overall thermal and electrical performance of the solar collector is considered as satisfactory and when operated simultaneously the overall performance is higher. In the same context, Pei G et al., [8] presented a novel heat pipe photovoltaic/thermal (PV/T) system that could simultaneously supply electrical and thermal energy was proposed. A dynamic model of the heat pipe PV/T system was presented, and a test rig was constructed. They showed that the average total first- and second law efficiencies of the PV/T system are 51.5% and 7.1%, respectively.

The PV/T solar collectors were also investigated on exergetic bases to compare the two kinds of energies, which are different in their quality. In 2010, Skin K et al., [9] presented a study dealing with the optimization of the number of collectors for PV/T hybrid active solar still for different heat capacity of water. It has been observed that the daily and exergy efficiency decreases linearly and nonlinearly with increase of water mass rates. In 2014, Sobhnamayan F et al., [10] presented an optimization study of a solar photovoltaic thermal (PV/T) water solar collector based on exergy concept. Genetic algorithm (GA) has been used to optimize the exergy efficiency of PV/T water collector. They showed that the maximum exergy efficiency is about 11.36%.

1.2. Objective of the Chapter

The primary objective of this chapter is to study the potential offered by the use of a PV/T solar collector (Figure 1) in Tunisian households to supply electricity and domestic hot water simultaneously. Our approach consists in appraising the thermal and the electric performances of the PV/T solar collector by achieving a series of experimentation under various Tunisian climatic conditions. The originality in our work is that it covers an energetic and exergetic study performed to obtain thermal and electrical parameters of the PV/T solar collector. The study presents a comparison between obtained results with literatures. The study presents also a comparison between the PV/T solar collector and the most popular water heating solar collectors and PV panel to confirm the improvement of the PV/T solar collector. The comparison was made on economic and availability bases.

Figure 1. The PV/T hybrid solar collector.

2. Experimental Study

The hybrid PV/T solar collector is designed to produce domestic hot water and to supply the electricity for a single family household. The PV cells of the PV/T solar collector used in our study (monocrystalline silicon) are encrusted adjacent to the surface of the cooper absorber. Involving the PV cells and the cooper absorber is fixed a layer of black tedlar–polyester–tellar (TPT) which assures the electrical insulation of the PV/T cells and improve the absorption of solar irradiation. A thermal insulation layer of polyurethane is positioned behind the cooper plate to prevent thermal loss by the back of the PV/T solar collector. The main physical property parameters of the PV/T solar collector are given in Table1.

In order to determine the thermal and the electric performances of the PV/T hybrid solar collector an experimental device was conceived and tested under outdoor field conditions in Borj cedria (North of Tunisia, Latitude 36°50’ N and Longitude 10°44’E) (Figure 2). The experimental device comprises mainly:

A PV/T hybrid solar collector mounted on a stand, oriented N-S, and tilted 40° N towards the south (Figure 1). The PV/T hybrid solar collector is connected through a water pump to a storage hot water tank with a capacity of 200 liters. Inside the storage tank is integrated an electric auxiliary heating equipments, a sliding valves and a flow-meters used to control the water mass flow rates during the experimental tests.

A HP multi-channel digital Data-logger connected to all the instruments and sensors was used for measuring experimental parameters (water temperatures, water mass flow rate, incident solar radiation. etc).PT100 sensors were used to measure water temperature of the inlet and outlet of the absorber. The PT100 was also used as the ambient temperature sensor. To record continuously the global irradiance a Kipp and Zonen pyranometer was mounted close to the PV/T collector surface.

A Muli-metre type Metrix was used to evaluate the instantaneous current and voltage outputs of the PV/T solar collector.

The experiments conducted in this chapter were carried out in July 2014 during which the solar irradiance intensity on the collector plane satisfies the experimental requirement. During the experimental study the rate of the incident solar radiation falling on to the PV/T solar collector as well as the temperature changes at: the inlet and the outlet of the PV/T solar collector, the PV cells, the output-current and the output-voltage delivered in open circuit mode were measured. Several days (12th, 13th, 14th and 15th of July 2014) are selected to present the experimental results.

In this chapter, two configurations of PV/T systems were studied. A PV/T solar water heating system functioning in passive mode (without water mass flow) and A PV/T solar water heating system functioning in active mode (with water mass flow). In active mode the PV/T solar water heating system needs a pump to circulate the water from the PV/T solar collector to hot water storage tank.

Table 1. PV/T hybrid solar collector characteristics

Specifications	Value
PV module type	Mono-crystalline silicon
Dimensions, mm^3	870x1640x105
Weight, kg	34,4
Sealing	Epdm and silicone
Thermal insolation coefficient, λ, W/mK$_i$	0.035
Cells number	72
Cells dimension, mm^2	125 x 125
Cells emissivity, ε_{cell}	0.95
Cells absorption coefficient, α_{cell}	0.85
Cells filling coefficient, β_{cell}	0.83
Cells temperature coefficient, β, °C^{-1}	0.0045
Absorber panel	Copper
Internal piping	Copper
Nominal power (W)	180
Nominal intensity (A)	4.64
Nominal voltage (V)	36.7
Sort-circuit current (A)	5.02
Sort-circuit voltage(V)	44.9

3. Energy and Exergy Performances Investigation

3.1. Energy Investigation

The useful heat gain, Q_{th}, is evaluated by means of the equation (1):

$$Q_{th} = \dot{m} C_p (T_o - T_i) \tag{1}$$

In order to specify the sharing of the incident solar radiation into the useful energy gain and to describes the optical losses effect on the thermal performance of the PV/T solar collector it is more appropriate to evaluate, Q_{th} by means of the Hottel–Whillier–Bliss equation [11]:

$$Q_{th} = A.F_R \left[(\tau\alpha)_{PV}.G - U_L (T_i - T_a) \right] \tag{2}$$

Knowing the values of F' andU_L, the heat removal factor F_R can be determined by using equation (3) [12]:

$$F_R = \frac{\dot{m}.C_p}{A.U_L}\left[1-\exp\left(-\frac{A.U_L.F'}{\dot{m}.Cp}\right)\right] \quad (3)$$

The instantaneous thermal steady state efficiency of the PV/T solar collector is determined by means of the equation (4):

$$\eta_{th} = \frac{\dot{m}.C_p\,(T_0 - T_i)}{G.A} \quad (4)$$

The thermal efficiency; η_{th}, of PV/T solar collector can also be calculated as a function of the ratio T_{av}-T_a/G:

$$\eta_{th} = F'(\tau\alpha)_{PV}\,K_\theta - a\frac{(T_{av}-T_a)}{G} - b\frac{(T_{av}-T_a)^2}{G} \quad (5)$$

The collector performance parameters ($F'(\tau\alpha)_{PV}\,K_\theta$, a(W/m^2 K) and b (W/m^2 K^2) are) are defined by the experimental study [12]. The incidence angle modifier (K_θ) for different angles of incidence (θ) are shown in Table 2 [13].

We establish also the average daily efficiency which is calculated by the relation (6):

$$\bar{\eta}_{th} = \frac{\int_{t_I}^{t_F} \dot{m}.C_p.(T_0(t)-T_i(t)).dt}{\int_{t_I}^{t_F} G(t).A.dt} \quad (6)$$

The electrical efficiency of the PV/T solar collector is given by the relation (7) [14]:

$$Q_{elec} = \eta_0\,[1-\beta(T_{cell} - T_{ref})] \quad (7)$$

where T_{ref} (25°C) is the reference temperature and β is temperature coefficient which represents the relation between the efficiency of the PV cells and the cell's temperature (β is about 0.0045 for silicon cells) [14, 15].

Table 2. Experimental values of the incidence angle modifier for different angles of incidence

θ	0	30	45	60	65	80
K_θ	1	0.98	0.94	0.80	0.73	0.40

The electrical efficiency of the PV/T solar collector evaluated at standards conditions (T_{ref} = 25°C and G_{max} = 1000W/m²) is given by the relation (8):

$$\eta_o = \frac{P_{elec}}{A.G} = \frac{U_{max}.I_{max}}{A.G} \tag{8}$$

3.2. Exergy Investigation

The exergy analysis (based on the second law analysis) is the most suitable method to get a clear vision on the PV/T solar collector efficiencies and on the degradation of energy during the thermal and the electrical conversion processes.

The heat transfer exergy rate, $\dot{E}x_{Q,sun}$, is the solar irradiance exergy rate which can be represented as [15, 16, 17]:

$$\dot{E}x_{Q,sun} = \dot{S}\left[1 - \frac{T_a}{T_{sun}}\right]$$

The heat transfer exergy rate includes the solar radiation intensity exergy rate $\dot{S} = G.A$. According to the Petela theorem, $\dot{E}x_{Q,sun}$ is also given by equation (9) [16, 17]:

$$\dot{E}x_{Q,sun} = \dot{S}\left[1-\frac{4}{3}(\frac{T_a}{T_{sun}})+\frac{1}{3}(\frac{T_a}{T_{sun}})^4\right] \tag{9}$$

The thermal exergy, $\dot{E}x_{th}$, is given by the equation (10):

$$\dot{E}x_{th} = (1-\frac{T_a}{T_{cells}}).Q_{th} \tag{10}$$

The electrical exergy, $\dot{E}x_{elec}$, is given by depends mainly on the incoming solar radiation and the PV modules temperature. $\dot{E}x_{elec}$ is calculated by using the equation [16, 17, 18]:

$$\dot{E}x_{elec} = \eta_0\left[1-\beta\left(T_{cell}-T_{ref}\right)\right] \tag{11}$$

The irreversibility rate, $\dot{I}$,includes the external exergy losses plus the internal exergy losses (exergy destructions) [16, 17, 18] is given by the equation (12):

$$\dot{I} = \dot{E}x_{loss} + \dot{E}x_{des} \tag{12}$$

where:

$\dot{E}x_{loss}$, caused by heat leakage rate is calculated by [16, 17, 18]:

$$\dot{E}x_{loss} = U_L.A.\left[1-(\frac{T_a}{T_{cell}})\right] \tag{13}$$

$\dot{E}x_{des}$ are equal to the product of reference environmental temperature to the entropy generation rate in control volume [16, 17, 18]:

$$\dot{E}x_{des} = T_{0.}\dot{S}_{gen} \tag{14}$$

The overall exergy efficiency of the PV/T solar collector is the sum of the thermal exergy ($\dot{E}x_{th}$) and electrical exergy ($\dot{E}x_{elec}$) of the system and the exergy efficiency can be defined as:

$$\Psi = \frac{\dot{E}x_{elec} + \dot{E}x_{th}}{\dot{E}_{x,sun}} \tag{15}$$

Table 3. Solar irradiation intensity and ambient temperature during the selected days of July 2014

Days	Solar irradiation intensity (W/m$^{2)}$	Ambient temperature (°C)
12th	400~1000	35.5~42
13th	390~1020	36.5~42.5
14th	420~1050	33.5~41.6
15th	380~1070	35~42.9

By substituting the values of $\dot{E}x_{th}$, $\dot{E}x_{elec}$ and $\dot{E}_{x,sun}$ in Eq. (15), the overall exergy efficiency of a PV/T solar collector results in:

$$\Psi = \frac{\left[1 - \beta\left(T_{cell} - T_{ref}\right)\right] V_m . I_m + (1 - \frac{T_a}{T_{cells}}) Q_{th}}{\dot{S}\left[1 - \frac{4}{3}(\frac{T_a}{T_{sun}}) + \frac{1}{3}(\frac{T_a}{T_{sun}})^4\right]} \tag{16}$$

4. PV/T Hybrid Solar Collector Performances

4.1. Thermal and Electric Outputs of the PV/T Solar Collector

In Table 3 are illustrated the solar radiation intensity and the ambient temperature arrays through the selected days of July 2014. it is seen that during the selected days of July (12th, 13th, 14th and 15th) the PV/T solar collector was exposed to solar radiation ranging from 380 and 1070W/m^2 and an ambient temperature in the array of 35~43°C.

In Figure 2 is the plotted the changes vs local time of the thermal energy supplied by the PV/T solar collector in both passive and active mode during the selected days of July 2014.It is seen that in passive mode the energy supplied by the PV/T solar collector ranges between 38.4 W/m^2 and 389 W/m^2. It is also seen that in active mode the energy supplied by the PV/T solar collector increase with water mass flow rate increases. Indeed for the water mass flow rates equals to 0.066 kg/s and to 0.083 kg/s the energy supplied by the PV/T stretches a maximum values of about 464.4 W/m^2 and 495.7 W/m^2, respectively. we noted also that the daily energy supplied by the PV/T solar collector is evaluated to about 2332.3 W/m^2 in passive mode whilst it growth in active mode to achieve the rates of 2768.5 W/m^2 and 3062.8 W/m^2 for the water mass flow equals 0.066 kg/s and 0.083 kg/s, respectively.

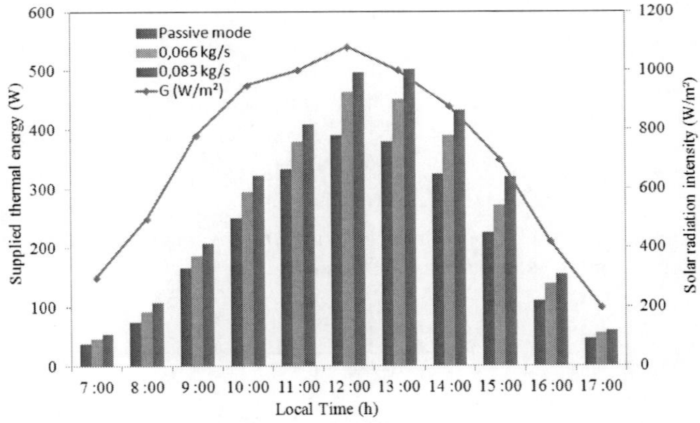

Figure 2. The thermal energy supplied by the PV/T solar collector in both passive and active modes during the selected days of July 2014.

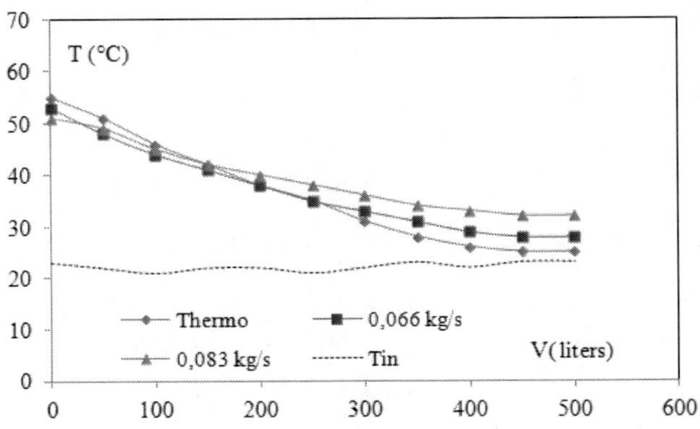

Figure 3. The quantities and the temperature of the water given by the PV/T solar collector (Ts) in both passive and active modes during the selected days of July 2014.

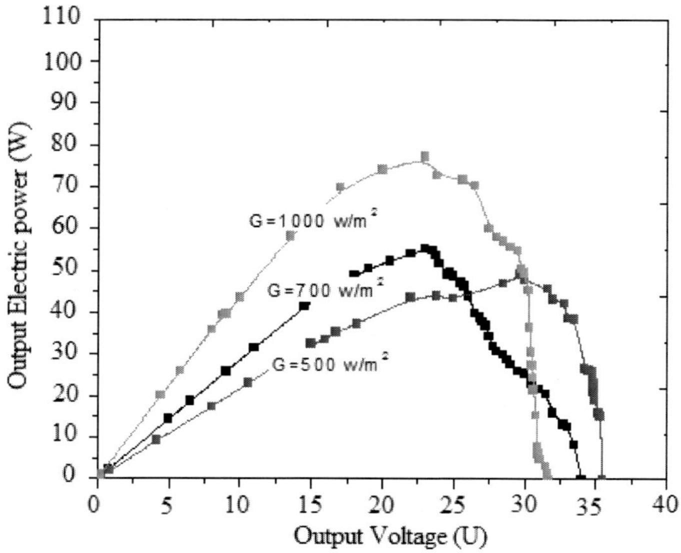

Figure 4. Output power vs voltage characteristic in passive mode for different values of solar radiation during the selected days of July 2014.

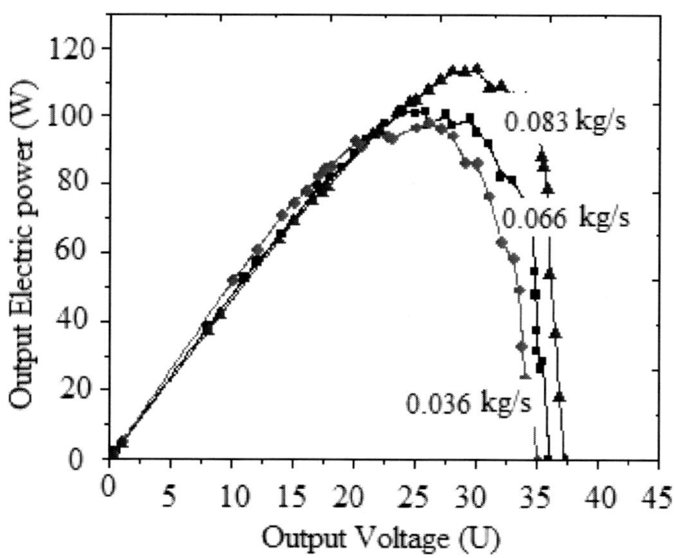

Figure 5. Output power vs voltage characteristic in active modes during selected days of July 2014.

In Figure 3 is represented the quantities (V) and the temperature of the water produced by the PV/T solar collector (Ts) in both passive and active modes. We found that the active mode improve considerably the amount of the supplied hot water. Indeed in passive mode the amount of the extracted water (V) was about 350 liters at an average temperature about 43°C. In active mode the extracted hot water enhances from 370 to 390 liters, at an average temperature of 45.5 and 48°C, for a mass flow rates equal respectively to 0.066 and 0.083 kg/s respectively.

In Figure 4 is demonstrated the electrical power, Pelec, produced in opened circuit by the PV/T solar collector vs output voltage U changes. The results are firstly depicted in passive mode during the selected days of July for several solar irradiation intensities (500, 700 and 1000 W/m²). We noted that Pelec growth with solar radiation increases while the short-circuit voltage (Ucc) decrease according to the solar radiation increases. Actuality for irradiation intensities equivalent to 500 and 1000 W/m² the output voltage (Vcc) drops from 36 to 31 V, respectively. In Figure 5 is represented the (Pelec-U) characteristics in active mode and for a solar radiation intensity equal to 1000 W/m². It should be noted that from 0 to 30 V (Pelec-U) are characterized by a linear growth. For voltage over 30 V, Pelec and U increases according to the water mass flow rates growth.

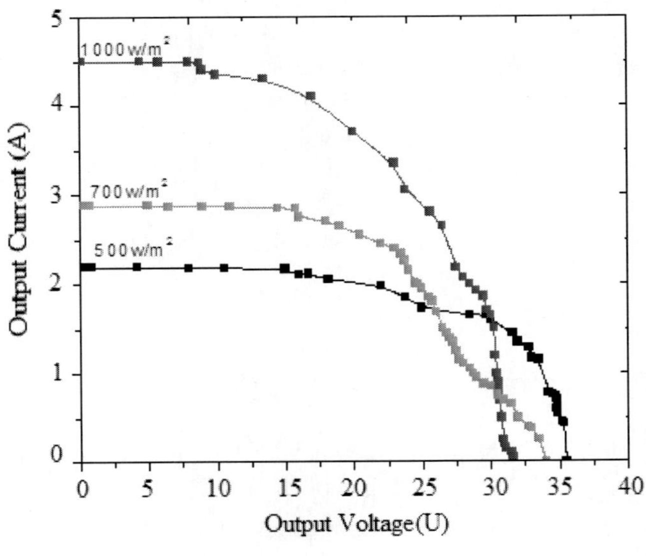

Figure 6.Output current vs output voltage in passive mode for different solar radiation intensity during the selected days of July 2014.

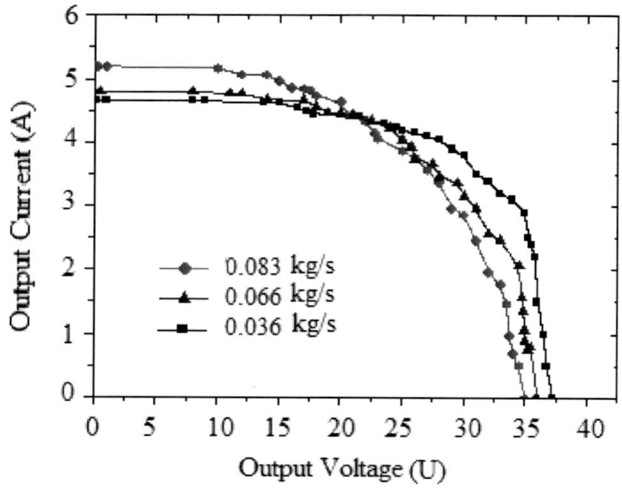

Figure 7.Output current vs output voltage in active mode during selected days of July 2014.

In Figure 6 is drown the current-voltage (I-U) characteristics of the PV/T solar collector in passive mode under different irradiance. It is seen that the short-circuit current (Icc) is proportional to solar radiation growth. Figure 8 demonstrated also that the short-circuit voltage (Vcc) is conversely proportional to solar radiation. Indeed, for the solar radiation 500, 700 and 1000 W/m², Ucc is respectively equals to 36, 34 and 32 V.

Figure 7, introduced the I-U characteristics of the PV/T solar collector in active mode for a maximum solar radiation of 1000 W/m². We deduce that the advantage of the hybrid system in active mode (With water mass flow) is obvious. Results show that Icc increase with mass flow rates increases even as Ucc decrease with mass flow rates.

4.2. Energy and Exergy Efficiency of the PV/T Solar Collector

The main result of the experimental test is the evaluation of the instantaneous efficiency η_{th} changes of the PV/T solar collector. In Table 4 are regrouped the characteristics parameters of the PV/T and the heat loss coefficient of the hot water storage tank (Equation5). In Figure 8 is illustrated the effect of the functioning mode on the instantaneous thermal efficiency of the PV/T solar collector during the selected days of July 2014. It is seen that in passive mode the instantaneous energy efficiencies of the PV/T solar collector vary between 12 and 36% from 07:00 to 12:00 and then decrease to 18%. It is also seen that in active mode the instantaneous energy efficiencies climb with the water mass flow rates enhances. It attains at 13:00 the maximum values of 39, 42 and 50%, for the water mass flow rates equal to 0.036, 0.066 and 0.083 kg/s, respectively.

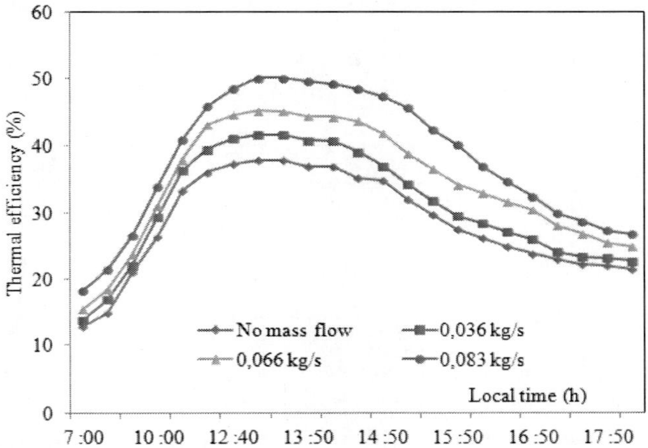

Figure 8. Variation of thermal efficiency vs local time in passive and active modes during the selected days of July 2014.

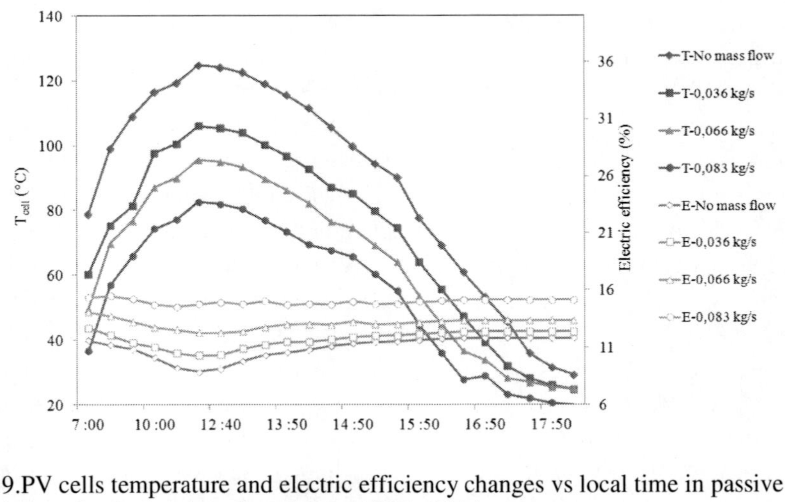

Figure 9.PV cells temperature and electric efficiency changes vs local time in passive and active modes during the selected days of July 2014.

Table 4. PV/T and hot water tank characteristics

Parameters	Value	Unit
Tested flow rates	0.027	kg/s
Intercept efficiency, ($F'(\tau\alpha)_{PV}\ K_{\theta}$)	0.486	%
First order efficiency coefficient, a	4.028	$W/m^2.K$
Second order efficiency coefficient, b	0.067	$W/m^2.K^2$
Hot water tank loss coefficient	1.6	$W/m^2.K$

Table 5. Average daily efficiency of the PV/T solar collector during the selected daysof July2014

Day	G (W/m^2)	Water mass flow rates (kg/s)	Q_{th}(W)	T_{cells} (°C)	$\overline{\eta_J}$
12th	845.30	Passive mode	458.9	86.51	39%
13th	865.50	0.036	514.9	70.75	42.7%
14th	845.30	0.066	535.4	62.33	46.5%
15th	845.30	0.083	580.2	52.60	49.3%

In Figure 9 are illustrated the variation of the solar cell Tcell temperature changes same as the electric efficiency in both passive and active mode during the selected days of July 2014 (12th, 13th, 14th and 15th). Results showed that in active mode (0.036 kg/s) the solar cells temperature, Tcell, rises (between 07:00 to 12:00) from 60 to 105°C with the increase of the solar radiation intensity and then drop to 30°C. It is also seen that the photovoltaic efficiency drop off from 13 to 11.2% with the increase of the solar radiation intensity. During the same period and for a mass flow rate equal to 0.066 kg/s it is obvious that while Tcell, growth from 50 to 96°C the electric efficiency decline from 14 to 12%. Besides for a more important mass flow rate (0.083 kg/s) Tcell, is in the array of 36~80°C from 07:00 to 12:00 whilst the electric efficiency is stabilized to about 15.7%. These results showed that the use of the PV/T solar collector in active mode ameliorates distinctly the significance of the instantaneous thermal efficiency. The active mode resulted also in Tcell drops by 17.73, 27.52, and 38.83% for a mass flow rates equals to 0.036, 0.066 and 0.083 kg/s, respectively (Table 5). The decrease of the solar cell temperature ameliorates the electric efficiency of the PV/T solar collector. The exergetic efficiency is a crucial parameter to evaluate the thermal and the electric potential of the PV/T solar collector. In table 6 is summarized the results of PV/T solar collector average daily exergy investigation. In Figure 10 is represented the instantaneous thermal energy efficiency as well as the instantaneous thermal exergy efficiency changes vs local time in both passive and active modes. It is seen that in passive mode the thermal energy and exergy efficiencies are in the arrays of 12 ~36% and 12 ~30%, respectively. Once a water mass flow of about 0.083 kg/s is assured inside the PV/T solar collector we establish that the thermal energy and the exergy efficiencies become more important. They range from 18 to 48% and from 12 to 41%, respectively. When compared to the exergy efficiency, we established that the thermal energy efficiency was always higher than net exergy efficiency. This was expected because for calculating the net energy efficiency, the quantity of the useful energy supplied by the PV/T solar collector was taken into account whereas the quality of this energy was neglected [23].

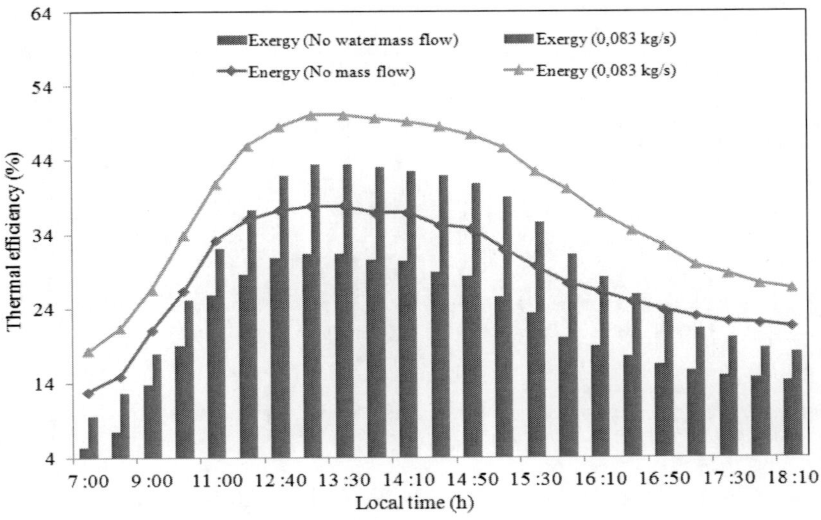

Figure 10. Variation vs local time of energy and exergy efficiency of the PV/T solar collector during the selected days of July 2014.

In Figure 11 is represented the electric exergy efficiency of the PV/T solar collector. It is seen that in passive mode the electric energy vary from 9.5 to 12% whereas in active mode (0.086 kg/s) it is approximately constant, about 15.5%. Figure 13 shows also that in passive mode the exergy electric efficiency ranges from 8.5 to 10.6% against an array of 12.5 and 14.8% obtained in active mode. We notes also that the difference between the electric energy and exergy is high as expected because the former is based on the open circuit voltage and short circuit current and also considers the thermal potential available on the PV/T surface whereas the latter considers only actual voltage and current produced and does not include thermal potential as it is considered to be a heat loss in this case. It is also attributed to the variation in the temperature difference between cell temperature and the ambient temperature and the power conversion efficiency which is slightly higher as compared to the exergy. The PV/T exergy efficiency was compared with other kind of PV/T solar collector that have been published (Table 7). It is seen that the PV/T solar collector exergy efficiency in active mode is affiliated to results obtained in literature.

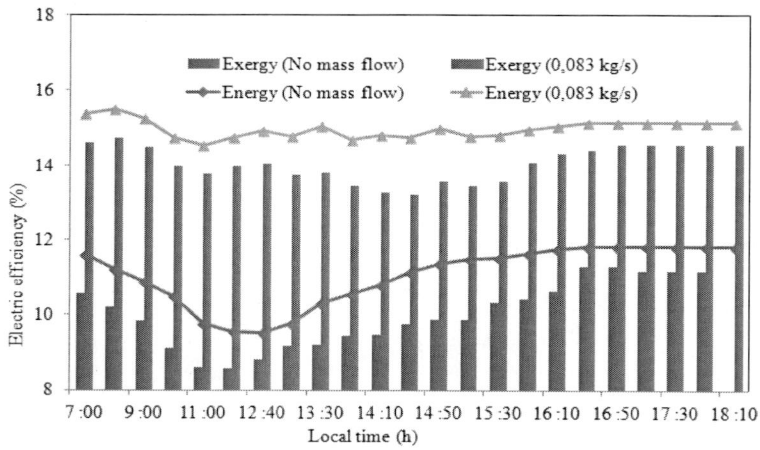

Figure 11. Electric exergy changes vs local time in passive and active modes during the days of July 2014.

Table 6. Exergy analysis of the PV/T hybrid solar collector

Day	Solar radiation exergy, $\dot{S}$ (W)	Water mass flow (kg/s)	Thermal exergy $\dot{E}x_{th}$ (W)	Electric exergy $\dot{E}x_{elec}$ (W)	Irreversibility rate, $\dot{I}$ (W)	Total exergy efficiency, Ψ (%)
12 July	1347,99	Passive mode	389,03	19,55	939,41	30.39
13 July	1331,88	0.036	458,30	19,15	854,43	35.84
14 July	1350,42	0.066	492,66	19,24	838,52	37.90
15 July	1389,42	0.083	502,46	20,14	814,26	39.32

Table 7. Exergy efficiency for some commercialized solar collector systems

Solar collector type	Exergy efficiency (%)
The coverless PV/T water collector (Fujisawa T and Tani T [18])	11–12.87%
The glazed PV/T water collector (Bosanac M et al., [19])	8–13%
The glazed PV/T water collector (Saitoh H et al., [20])	13.3%

4.3. PV/T Hybrid Solar Collector vs Commercialized Solar Systems

The thermal performances of the PV/T solar collector were compared with the most commercial domestic water heaters in Tunisia (Evacuated tube collector (ETC) and flat-plate solar collector (FPC)) intended to produce 200 l of hot water daily. The electric outputs of the PV/T solar collector are compared to the electric outputs of a PV panel available in Tunisian market destined to produce electric energy. The thermal efficiency, η_{th} (ETC and FPC), electric efficiency, η_{elect} (PV panel), and economic profitability were analyzed and compared for each system on the base of experiments achieved during comparable climatic conditions.

Table 8. Comparison of the cost and the payback times between FPC, ETC, PV panel and the PV/T solar collector

	PV/T	FPC	ETC	PV panel
System cost, $	1370	940	1100	638
The annual energy gain, kW h.m^{-2}	450	690	720	175.2
Installation cost, $	20	20	20	20
Upholding cost, $	40	40	60	50
Electricity saving, kW h/year	1600	1316	1459	106.47
Cost payback (based on electric water heater), years	10	8	10	6

It is found that in passive mode the PV/T solar collector carried out during hot months an average daily thermal performance, η_{th}, about 39%, whilst the ETC and FPC average daily thermal efficiency of about 45.6 and 58.8%, respectively [13, 21, 22]. We noted also that the PV/T exergy efficiency vary between 12 and 35% whilst the thermal exergy efficiency of the ETC and the

FPC varies between 13 and 40% and between 16 and 45%, respectively [21, 22]. The comparison analysis shows that the PV/T solar collector exergy efficiency is quite good compared to the ETC and FPC solar collectors. We concluded that the PV/T solar collector has a satisfactory performance therefore it can partly cover the thermal needs of a typical Tunisian family.

We have also compared the electric efficiency, η_{elect}, of the PV/T solar collector to a PV panel with the same dimensions during comparable climatic conditions. Results showed that due to the water mass flow the PV/T solar collector has an important electric efficiency, η_{elect}, in the array of 11 and 13.8% while the η_{elect} of the PV panel ranges between 10.8 and 12% [23, 24]. The PV/T exergy electric efficiency was also compared with PV panel exergy efficiency. Results showed that the PV/T exergy efficiency in active mode between 12 and 35% whilst the thermal exergy electric efficiency of the PV panel ranges between 13 and 40% [25]. We presume that the PV/T solar collector presents an important electric efficiency and exergy compared to PV panels.

An economic comparison between PV/T hybrid solar collector, FPC, ETC and PV panel was performed (Table 8). The energy payback was calculated by considering 20 years as the as the estimated lifespan of the PV/T solar collector the ETC, FPC and PV panel on the basis of selling price of 1 kWh of electricity in Tunisia which costs 0.041 $ [26]. The energy payback for each system was estimated by considering the number of years needed by each solar installation to save as much energy as its energy invested. Investment profitability analysis of the FPC and the ETC are presented by the authors in an earlier study [26]. A detailed economic analysis of hybrid PV thermal solar systems is presented by Tripanagnostopoulos Y et al., [27]. The annual savings were estimated considering negligible energy losses and 1% of the present cost was taken for the estimation of maintenance and repair costs of all solar collectors [28, 29]. It is found that the costs per square meter area of the FPC system and ETC system are respectively of about 940 $ and 1100 $ as against the cost of about 1370 $ of the PV/T solar collector. Further we note that the cost per square meter area of the PV panel (300 W and 72 cells) is of about 638 $. Although, an extra cost of 237.803 $ is required for the PV panel installation and exploitation. We notice that the energy payback period depends noticeably of substituted conventional water heating systems. For the FPC, the annual electricity saving and payback period is of about 1316 kW h/year and 8 years based on electric water. For the ETC the annual electricity saving and payback period is assumed to 1459 kW h/year and 10 years based on electric water heater. Regarding the PV/T solar collector, the annual electricity saving and payback period are of about 106.5 kW h/year and 10 years as against an annual electricity saving and a payback period of about 106.5 kW h/year and 6 years for a PV panel of 72 cells and having the same area [6, 30].

SUMMARY

This chapter presents the investigation achieved to reveal the potential offered by the integration off PV/T hybrid solar collector in Tunisian households. Numerous experiments were carried out in order to evaluate the electric and thermal performances of the PV/T solar collector. An energetic and exergetic analysis under Tunisian's climate conditions was also presented to appraise the impacts of climate conditions and operating parameters on the PV/T electric and thermal efficiencies. The remarking points could be outlined as below. As given in the results section, PV cells temperature can increase up to 120°C depending significantly on outside parameters, mostly affected by ambient temperature and global solar radiation.

Overall results show that using PV/T solar collector in active mode (With water mass flow) present obvious advantages. Indeed in active mode the amount of the supplied thermal energy is estimated to about 3kW/m² against about 2.33 kW/m² of energy in passive mode. Besides the extracted water in active mode, about 370~390 liters, at a temperature of 45.2~ 48°C, is more significant than the water supplied in passive mode which is about 350 liters at an average temperature of 43°C. The PV/T solar collector can yield improved thermal energy performances due to achieved PV cells cooling. Hence the declines of the PV cells temperature contribute to improve the thermal and electric energy outputs. We found that in active mode the thermal efficiency of the PV/T solar collector is significantly ameliorated compared to the passive mode. Other than the thermal efficiency, removing waste heat away from the PV/T collectors can enhance the electric efficiency of the PV/T solar collector. It is seen that in passive mode the electric energy vary from 9.5 to 12% whereas in active mode it is about 15.5%. It is also established that the thermal exergy efficiency of the PV/T solar collector in active mode (12 to 41%) was more important than in passive mode (6 to 30%). The results showed also that in active mode the exergy electric efficiency is also ameliorated compared to the passive mode. The PV/T solar collector energetic and exergtic thermal efficiencies are quite good compared to the ETC and FPC solar collectors. We founded also that the electric outputs of the PV/T solar collector are also prevalently enhanced compared to the electric outputs of a PV panel available in Tunisian market.

An assessment between PV/T hybrid solar collector, FPC, ETC and PV panel based techno-economic analysis was also carried out. We presume that the cost payback of the PV/T water heating system (10 years) almost the same cost payback of the ETC and FPC solar collector. However it is more important than PV panels (6 years). Although the thermal energy gain in the PV/T hybrid solar collector makes it economically more attractive compared to the PV panels. However, if there is a demand for heat only, having a solar thermal system would be more appropriate due to greater thermal performance and better economic feasibility of solar thermal systems. In case of electricity demand only, the PV/T solar collector is more suitable due to its electric performances. It is also to mention that incentives towards PV/T solar systems significantly affect their economic feasibility. Since PV/T systems do have an aspect strongly related to environmental and social responsibility, policies toward encouragement of implementations and extending use in Tunisian household's applications.

REFERENCES

Anand S, Joshi ID, Bale V R. Performance analysis of photovoltaic systems: A review. *Renew Sust Energ Rev* 2009:13: 1884–1897.

Ayompe LM, Duffy A, Mc Keever M, Conlon M, McCormack SJ. Comparative field performance study of flat plate and heat pipe evacuated tube collectors (ETCs) for domestic water heating systems in a temperate climate. *Energy* 2011:36: 3370-3378.

Bosanac M, Sorensen B, Ivan K, Sorensen H, Bruno N, Jamal B. Photovoltaic/Thermal Solar Collectors and Their Potential in Denmark, Final Report, *EFP Project* 2003: 1713/00-0014.

Bahaidarah H, Subhan A, Gandhidasan P, Rehman S. Performance evaluation of a PV (photovoltaic) module by back surface water cooling for hot climatic conditions. *Energy* 2013: 59: 445-453.

Christopher Gross. Le marché photovoltaïque en Tunisie : Situation actuelle et perspectives. Juillet 2013.

Dubey S, Tay AAO. Testing of two different types of photovoltaic-thermal (PVT) modules with heat flow pattern under tropical climatic conditions. *Energy Sus Dev* 2013;17: 1–12.

Duffie JA, Beckman WA. Solar Engineering of Thermal Processes, Second edition 1991.

Fischer S, Heidemann W, Muller-Steinhagen H, Perers B, Bergquist P, Hellstrom B. Collector test method under quasi-dynamic conditions according to the European Standard EN 12975-2. *Sol Energy* 2004:76: 117–123.

Erzat E, Mustafa I, Fuat E. An experimental study on energy generation with a photovoltaic (PV)– solar thermal hybrid system. *Energy* 2008: 33:1241–1245.

Fujisawa T, Tani T. Annual exergy evaluation on photovoltaic-thermal hybrid collector. *Sol Energ Mat Sol C*1997 :47: 135–148.

Joshi AS, Dincer I, Reddy BV. Energetic and exergetic analyses of a photovoltaic system. Proceedings of the Canadian Society for Mechanical Engineering (CSME) Forum 2008, Paper No: 1569103179: 5–8.

Jahangiri S, Mamouri H, Gholami D, Ghiasi M, Shafii MB, Shiee Z. Experimental investigation of the effect of using thermosyphon heat pipes and vacuum glass on the performance of solar still. *Energy* 2014:75: 501-507.

Joshi AS, Tiwari A, Tiwari GN, Dincer I, Reddy BV. Performance evaluation of a hybrid photovoltaic thermal (PV/T) (glass-to-glass) system. *Int J Therm Sci* 2009:48:154–164.

Haurant P, Menezo C, Gaillard L, Dupeyrat P. Dynamic numerical model of a high efficiency PV–T collector integrated into a domestic hot water system. *Sol Energy* 2015: 111: 68–81.

Hazami M, Kooli S, Naili N, Farhat A. Long-term performances prediction of an evacuated tube solar water heating system used for single-family households under typical Nord-African climate (Tunisia). *Sol Energy* 2013:94: 283–298.

Hepbasli A. A key review on exergetic analysis and assessment of renewable energy resources for a sustainable future. *Renew Sust Energ Rev* 2008:12: 593–661.

Hazami M, Naili N, Attar I, Farhat A. Solar water heating systems feasibility for domestic requests in Tunisia: Thermal potential and economic analysis. *Energ Convers Manage* 2013:76: 599–608.

Kalogirou S. Use of TRNSYS for modeling and simulation of a hybrid pv thermal solar system for Cyprus. *Ren Energy* 2001;23:247–60.

Mohd NAB, Mahmod O, Mahadzir HD, Norain A. Manaf, Hasila J. Design concept and mathematical model of a bi-fluid photovoltaic/thermal (PV/T) solar collector. *Renew Energ* 2014:67: 153-164.

Patrick D, Christope M, Harry W, Mathias R. Improvement of PV module optical properties for PV-thermal hybrid collector application. *Sol EnergMat Sol C* 2011:95: 2028-2036.

Park KE, Kang GH, Kim HI, Yu GJ, Kim JT. Analysis of thermal and electrical performance of semi-transparent photovoltaic (PV) module. *Energy* 2010:35: 2681–2687.

Pei G, Fu H, Zhu H, Ji J. Performance study and parametric analysis of a novel heat pipe PV/T system. *Energy* 2012:37: 384-395.

Sarhaddi F, Farahat S, Ajam H, Behzadmehr A. Exergetic performance assessment of a solar photovoltaic thermal (PV/T) air collector. *EnergBuildings* 2010: 42: 2184–2199.

Saitoh H, Hamada Y, Kubota H, Nakamura M, Ochifuji K, Yokoyama S, Nagano K. Field experiments and analyses on a hybrid solar collector. *Appl Therm Eng* 2003:23: 2089–2105.

Sujala B, Gopi Krishna K, Seung-Hee E, Jae-Heun Oh, Dae Hyun K. *Energy* 2013: 61:272-282.

Sujala B, Gopi KK, Seung-Hee E, Jae-Heun O, Dae HK. Comparative study of photovoltaic and thermal solar systems with different storage capacities: Performance evaluation and economic analysis. *Energy* 2013:61: 272-282.

Shiv K, Tiwari GN, Gaur MK. Development of empirical relation to evaluate the heat transfer coefficients and fractional energy in basin type hybrid (PV/T) active solar still. *Desalination* 2010:250: 214–221.

Sobhnamayan F, Sarhaddi F, Alavi MA, Farahat S, Yazdanpanahi J. Optimization of a solar photovoltaic thermal (PV/T) water collector based on exergy concept. *Renew Energ* 2014:68: 356-365.

Tomas M. Performance and economic analysis of hybrid PVT collectors in solar DHW system. *Energ Procedia* 2014:48: 150 – 156.

Tripanagnostopoulos Y, Souliotis M, Battisti R, Corrado A. Energy, cost and LCA results of PV and hybrid PV/T solar systems. *ProgressPhotovoltaics: Res Appl* 2005;13:234–50.

BIOGRAPHICAL SKETCH

Majdi HAZAMI

Affiliation: Laboratoire des Procédés Thermique, Centre de Recherches des Technologies de l'Energie.

Education:

2002-2003/2007-2008: Thesis of Doctorate

Name of Faculty: Faculty of Sciences of Tunis

Applied Mechanics of Fluids and Thermal Transfer

Thesis title: Experimental and numerical study of the phenomenon of thermal energy storage and destocking by using capillary polypropylene heat exchangers.

Mention: High honors

1998-2001: Master

Name of Faculty: Faculty of Sciences of Tunis

Specialty: Applied Mechanics of Fluids and Thermal Transfer,

Master title: Cooling of the Salammbô museum aquariums.

1993-1994/1997-1998: High School Graduation Diploma

Name of Faculty: Faculty of Sciences of Bizerte

Specialty: Physics

Mention: Acceptable

1997-1998: Bachelor of Experimental Science degree

Name of School: 20 march scool Menzel Bourguiba

Mention: Acceptable

Business Address: Hammam Lif, B.P. 95, 2050. Tunis. Tunisia.

Research and Professional Experience:

2003-2006: Contractual assistant

Laboratory and center name: Laboratory of Thermal Proceeds, Research Center of Energy Technologies.

Main activities and responsibilities: Scientific research

2006-2007: Contractual assistant

Preparatory Institue of Engineers studies of Tunis.

Main activities and responsibilities: Teaching

Practical course: Geometric optic, mechanic, thermal transfer, electric, magnetic

Level: 1st year License in Applied Industry and Food processing

2007-2010: Assistant (permanent)

Laboratory of Thermal Proceeds, Research Center of Energy Technologies.

Main activities and responsibilities: Scientific research

2007-2010: Assistant (vacation)

Preparatory Institue of Engineers studies of Tunis.

Main activities and responsibilities: Teaching

Practical course: Geometric optic, mechanic, thermal transfer, electric, magnetic

Level: 1st year License in Applied Industry and Food processing

2010: Assistant Professor (permanent)

Laboratory of Thermal Proceeds, Research Center of Energy Technologies.

Main activities and responsibilities: Scientific research

2010-2011: Assistant Professor (Vacation)

Preparatory Institute of Engineers studies of Tunis.

Main activities and responsibilities: Teaching

Practical course: Geometric optic, mechanic, thermal transfer, electric, magnetic

Level: 1st year License in Applied Industry and Food processing

2014-2015: Assistant Professor (Vacant)

Faculty of Sciences of Bizerte

Main activities and responsibilities: Teaching

Practical course: Lipid Technology

Level: 1st year Professional master in HVAC and Energy management

Publications Last 3 Years:

1. MajdiHazami, Sami Kooli, Nabiha Naili, Abdelhamid Farhat, Long-term performances prediction of an evacuated tube solar water heating system used for single-family households under typical Nord-African climate (Tunisia), Solar Energy 94 (2013) 283–298.
2. MajdiHazami, Nabiha Naili, Issam Attar, Abdelhamid Farhat, Solar water heating systems feasibility for domestic requests in Tunisia: Thermal potential and economic analysis, Energy Conversion and Management 76 (2013) 599–608.
3. Nabiha Naili, MajdiHazami, Issam Attar, Abdelhamid Farhat, In-field performance analysis of ground source cooling system with horizontal ground heat exchanger in Tunisia, Energy 61 (2013) 319-331.

4. Nabiha Naili, Issam Attar, MajdiHazami, Abdelhamid Farhat, First in situ operation performance test of ground source heat pump in Tunisia, Energy Conversion and Management 75 (2013) 292–301.
5. Issam Attar, Nabiha Naili, Nahla Khalif, Majdi.Hazami, Abdelhamid Farhat, Parametric and numerical study of a solar system for heating a greenhouse equipped with a buried exchanger, Energy Conversion and Management 70 (2013) 163–173.
6. Nabiha Naili, Majdi Hazami, Sami Kooli, Abdelhamid Farhat, Energy and exergy analysis of horizontal ground heat exchanger for hot climatic condition of northern Tunisia, Geothermics 53 (2015) 270–280.
7. Farah Mehdaoui, Majdi Hazami, Nabiha Naili, Abdelhamid Farhat, Energetic performances of an optimized passive Solar Heating Prototype used for Tunisian buildings air-heating application, Energy Conversion and Management 87 (2014) 285–296.

In: Tunisia
Editor: Eunice Wagner
ISBN: 978-1-53610-061-7
© 2016 Nova Science Publishers, Inc.

Chapter 6

ARE CURRENT WASTEWATER TREATMENTS ENOUGH TO AVOID PUBLIC HEALTH PROBLEMS IN TUNISIA

Imen Ouardani[1,2], Mahjoub Aouni[2] and Jesús L. Romalde[1,*]

[1]Departamento de Microbiología y Parasitología.
CIBUS-Facultad de Biología.
Universidade de Santiago de Compostela. Spain
[2]Laboratoire des Maladies Transmissibles et Substances Biologiquement Actives. Faculté de Pharmacie. Université de Monastir. Tunisia

ABSTRACT

The reuse of treated wastewater in irrigation and to refill the aquifer became a common strategy in Tunisia to palliate the lack of water resources. However, sewage treatment processes currently used are only partially effective to remove viruses and consequently discharge of contaminated treated wastewater is a potential source of viral infections. Hepatitis A virus (HAV), hepatitis E virus (HEV), norovirus (NoV), rotavirus (RV), enterovirus (EV), astrovirus (AsV), sapovirus (SaV), adenovirus (AdV) and aichi virus (AiV) are, among enteric viruses, the

[*] Corresponding author: Departamento de Microbiología y Parasitología. CIBUS-Facultad de Biología. Universidade de Santiago de Compostela. Santiago de Compostela 15782, Spain Email: jesus.romalde@usc.es.

major waterborne pathogens, predominantly transmitted via the faecal-oral route, and important agents implicated in gastroenteritis or hepatitis outbreaks. They are released in large quantities in raw wastewater and can survive for long periods in several environments which present an important public health hazards. Due to their persistence and low infectious dose, enteric viruses can easily infect people via water or food. Although Tunisia is considered as an endemic country for enteric viruses, routine surveillance of viral wastewater quality is not performed and data on viral epidemiology are limited. In this review we provide an overview on the prevalence of the most common enteric viruses in wastewater from different regions of Tunisia including socioeconomic data and seasonal distribution when available. Indeed, efficiency of different wastewater treatment processes for viral reduction is discussed in order to evaluate the risk associated to the wastewater in the country. Data show that RV, HAV, EV and NoV are constantly present in both raw and treated wastewater with high prevalence. Differences in the incidence of these viruses in wastewater within the country are linked to variations in socioeconomic and sanitary conditions, geographic area and climate. We describe also the genetic diversity of multiple pathogenic enteric viruses in sewage. Different viral reduction rates are observed demonstrating the difficulty of the present biological treatments to provide virus-free wastewater effluents. This review contributes to the understanding of the epidemiology of enteric viruses in Tunisia and underlines the need of an environmental surveillance program and official viral controls for treated wastewater. Therefore, efforts should focus on the enhancing of sewage treatment technologies to avoid a social and public health hazard.

Keywords: wastewater, enteric viruses, treatment, prevalence, STP

Introduction

Because of their arid and semi-arid climate, the Middle East and North Africa (MENA) region has only 1% of global freshwater resources (Qadir et al., 2007). The countries of the MENA depend mainly on seasonal rainfall, have very few rivers and and often rely on aquifers, which some of them are non-renewable (Qadir et al., 2010). Consequently, their economies are much more sensitive to the way that water is extracted, transported and consumed than are the economies of other regions (Jagannathan et al., 2009). In addition, with the constant increasing demand of water in different sectors including agriculture, which is the main consumer of water, some of these countries are suffering from hydraulic stress and are threatened by water scarcity (Allan,

2001). Hence, most of MENA countries had established processes of integrated water resource management, which advocated new approaches for the assessment, management, and development of freshwater resources. Among these strategies, the increase of treated wastewater reuse rates, in both agriculture and industry, has been proposed as the best alternative to preserve as long as possible natural water resources in the driest part of the world (Bahri, 2008).

Tunisia is a country of MENA region, located in the extreme north of Africa, and influenced by three types of climate: Mediterranean climate in the north, semi-arid climate in the central part and desertic climate in the south. Thus, the annual rainfall is on average of 594 mm in the North, 289 mm in the Centre and only 156 mm in the extreme South (Neubert and Benabdallah, 2003). This situation made Tunisia a country with relatively limited renewable water resources, having unequalled geographical distribution. Faced to the continuous increase in water demand, due to the rapid population growth coupled with industrialization, urbanization and agricultural intensification, the country recognizes a constant drop in the availability of water resources.

As economy of Tunisia is mainly based on agriculture, irrigation consumes about 83% of the total volume of distributed water. Therefore, according to the National Sanitation Office (ONAS), a treated wastewater reuse program in agriculture, irrigation of green spaces and aquifer recharge, has been launched from the early 1980s in order to preserve water resources. However, irrigation with treated wastewater back to the year 1965 with the first perimeter of the Soukra irrigated with treated wastewater from the treatment plant of Charguia. Thanks to initiatives taken by the State, since 1989, to encourage the use of this source and to minimize its release in the aquatic environment (Bahri and Brissaud, 1996), the policy of treated wastewater reuse was enhanced and irrigated areas have undergone significant evolution.). The increase in wastewater production, mainly due to the urban population growth as well as the increase of public sewer connection rate, raised subsequently the annual productive reuse of treated wastewater in agriculture, reaching 120 million m^3 in 1996 and 210 million m^3 in 2010 (Ministère de l'Agriculture de Tunisie, 1998). From 2015, 28% of these waters (60 million m^3) are reused for irrigation of 8150 hectares of agricultural areas, including citrus fruits, olives, peaches, pears, apples, pomegranates, grain and industrial crops, 1040 hectares of golf courses and 450 hectares of green spaces.

However, regulations regarding the discharge and reuse of wastewater were implemented by the Tunisian Republic (Journal Officiel de la République Tunisienne, 2010):

- Decree n° 85-86 (02-01-1985) regulates wastewater discharges in the receiving environment by setting the terms for their release from wastewater treatment plants (STPs). This decree stipulates that treated wastewater must meet the criteria established by the standard NT 106.02, approved in July 20, 1989 (INNORPI, 1989a), which regulates the discharge conditions and defines the quality of effluents according to the receiving environment (sea, lakes, rivers...). In fact, reduction values required for wastewater discharges are evaluated according to physicochemical parameters, including biochemical oxygen demand (BOD), chemical oxygen demand (COD), total suspended solids (TSS) and total phosphorus and nitrogen, bacteriological parameters, several heavy metals and some organic micro-pollutants.
- Decree n° 93-2447 (13-12-1993) specifies modalities of treated wastewater reuse in agriculture by limiting the use for only crops irrigation except vegetables, whether eaten raw or cooked (Bahri and Brissaud, 1996). It sets also the frequency of analysis for physicochemical parameters (once a month), trace elements (once every six months), and bacteriological analysis for the research of helminth eggs (once every two weeks). To be reused, treated wastewater quality must follow the standard NT106.03, approved in June 1989 (INNORPI, 1989b), which supervises the reuse of treated wastewater in agriculture in order to avoid a negative impact on public health.

Despite all the efforts made by the State to improve the quality of treated wastewater, there is neither regulation or survey program for viruses. In addition, reduced values of various parameters do not address indication of behaviour of highly stable pathogens (like viruses), and current methods of wastewater treatment are not very effective against them, which subsequently cause viral contamination of the environment. The lack of virological analysis and the inability to provide virus-free treated wastewater constitute a potential hazard to public health since the government is investigating, through pilot projects, the reuse of treated wastewater for aquifers recharge, irrigation of forests and highways, as well as for industrial use.

STPs represent the main reservoir and a spreading mechanism of all kinds of pollutants and a large variety of enteric viruses transported by urban wastewater, especially in cases of sewage system dysfunction. Tunisia was the first among Mediterranean countries to use STPs, implemented initially in big cities in order to protect citizens' health and promote their living, then on coastal areas, wetlands, small and medium communities and industrial areas. Actually, most STPs are located along the coast to protect water resources and fragile ecosystems and to improve the quality of bathing water of coastal resorts (Bahri and Brissaud, 1996).

Many wastewater treatment processes were therefore developed and employed prior to discharge wastewater into the natural environment. The process starts with primary elimination of the bulky waste by screening, followed by secondary biological or physicochemical treatment and completed with tertiary treatment to refine the final quality of treated wastewater. Actually, Tunisia utilises both primary and biological secondary treatment processes in almost all STPs (Qadir et al., 2010). A range of biological wastewater treatment options is used, including activated sludge and lagoon processes, but treatment level varies between urban and rural areas (Qadir et al., 2010). However, with the increase in urban population, some STPs do not have the capacity to process such large volumes and consequently, retention times for wastewater become too short to be effective. Therefore, the government efforts are currently focused on the upgrade to tertiary level treatment (Melhem et al., 2014).

Human sewage can contain a wide variety of different viruses, routinely introduced in the environment through the discharge of raw and treated wastewater. The most important human pathogenic viruses are enterically transmitted and able to cause a wide spectrum of illnesses. They are transmitted primarily via faecal-oral route, either by direct contact form person to person or indirectly through consumption of contaminated water or food, being the origin of many epidemics in developing countries. However, other modes of transmission, such as sexual, parenteral and zoonosis, can be also considered. Enteric viruses are very small microorganisms, about 25 to 220 nm, non enveloped and thus very stable in the environment (Bosch et al., 2008). As obligate intracellular parasites, these viruses are unable to multiply outside the cell host and remain inert for a long period until they are ingested by accident. Once replicated, they are shed in very high numbers in the faeces of infected persons, up to 10^{11} viral particles per gram of stool, reaching then wastewater treatment plants before to be released in the environment. In water, they are preferentially adsorbed to settleable suspended solids (clay, sand, sediment) that protect them against environmental stressors, allowing their concentration in sediments and preserving their infectivity. Due to their great resistance to physical and chemical agents, their low infectious dose, their high concentrations in feaces (Patel et al., 2009), enteric viruses can, through the discharge of wastewater, easily contaminate soil, water and food.

Enteric viruses are classified into three main groups according to pathologies they produce in humans. The first group includes mainly norovirus (NoV), rotavirus (RV), sapovirus (SV), adenovirus (AdV), astroviruses (AsV) and aichi virus (AiV), causing acute gastroenteritis. The second group includes hepatitis A virus (HAV) and hepatitis E virus (HEV) that are responsible of acute enterically transmitted hepatitis. Enteroviruses (EV), members of the third group, can migrate to other organs after replication in the intestinal tract, causing lesions of the central nervous system, gastrointestinal tract infections, respiratory infections, mucocutaneous infections and conjunctivitis (Koopmans and Duizer, 2004).

In Tunisia, little is know about prevalence of these viruses in wastewater and only major pathogenic agents, such as HAV, HEV, NoV, RV, EV and AiV were studied.

Hepatitis A Virus

Hepatitis A virus (HAV) is the only representative of the genus *Hepatovirus* in the family *Picornaviridae* and the etiological agent of acute hepatitis A (Bosch et al., 2008; Lu et al., 2004). It is a linear single-stranded ribonucleic acid virus (RNA), non-enveloped with approximately 7.5 kb genome, protected within an icosahedral capsid (Pintó et al., 2012). HAV has been classified into six genotypes (I to VI) (Costa-Mattioli et al., 2002; Lu et al., 2004; Cristina and Costa-Mattioli, 2007) and a single serotype (Sanchez et al., 2002; Hollinger and Emerson, 2007; Perez-Sautu et al., 2011). The first three genotypes (I, II and III), subdivided into two subtypes A and B (Byun et al., 2001), were isolated from humans while the other three (IV, V and VI) were isolated only from simian species who developed a hepatitis A-like disease (Nainan et al., 1991; Tsarev et al., 1991).

HAV is more resistant in the water environment than other picornavirus: It is found in tap water after 60 days (Enriquez et al., 1995) and in the sterile mineral water after 89 days (Debord and Buisson, 1998). It can also survive for up 8 weeks in groundwater (Sobsey et al., 1989), over 6 weeks in the river waters (Springthorpe et al., 1993), and up to 30 weeks in sea water (Crance et al., 1998).

Waterborne transmission of HAV may occur in different ways, either by consumption of contaminated water (Kukkula et al., 1997) or during recreational activities (Fleisher et al., 1996). Since HAV is excreted in faeces in a large number of copies (up to 10^{11} copies/g of faeces) (Costafreda et al., 2006; Pinto et al., 2012), transmission is facilitated by poor sanitation (Jacobsen and Koopman, 2005). Furthermore, the use of contaminated wastewater in irrigation of green areas or in agriculture may also be the origin of several cases of hepatitis A (Koopmans and Duizer, 2004; Bosch et al., 2008). In addition, their release in seawater presents a potential risk to public health, given that the virus is concentrated by filter-feeder organisms such as mussels and oysters and their consumption, either raw or undercooked, is associated sometimes in the appearance of large scale epidemics (Costafreda et al., 2006; Pintó et al., 2009; Rodríguez-Lázaro et al., 2012). Secondarily, food washed with contaminated water and eaten raw may constitute a source of infection.

In Tunisia, hepatitis A remains endemic, with high/intermediate ranking (Letaief et al., 2005; Rezig et al., 2008; Gharbi-Khelifi et al., 2007; Melhem et al., 2014; Ouardani et al., 2015), occurring primarily in young children at high rates. HAV serologic studies conducted in the 2000s in different regions, depending on age, have shown high prevalence, in young children aged under 10 years (44% - 84%) as well as children aged from 10 to 15 years (59% - 91%) and teens aged from 16 to 25 years (83% - 92%). The prevalence of infection varies between urban and rural areas, according to the development of regions, hygienic conditions and sewage facilities (Letaief et al., 2005; Rezig et al., 2008). However, in many urban areas, hepatitis incidence has not been reduced although the improvement of hygiene conditions in those areas. As hepatitis A disease may be symptomatic or not, detectable HAV in wastewater would provide an important overview of its spread in the general population (Ouardani et al., 2015). Several reports, conducted in the country on raw and treated wastewater samples, showed high HAV rates ranging between 46% and 68.3% and high HAV loads up to 1.68×10^9 genome copies(GC)/L, suggesting the important role of this source of viruses in the transmission of the disease (Gharbi-Khelifi et al., 2007; Béji-Hamza et al., 2014; Ouardani et al., 2015, 2016).

Despite of the potential public health hazard linked to the lack of good sanitation and the use of contaminated treated sewage, few studies have been carried out in Tunisia on the seasonal and geographical distribution of HAV in the environment. In these reports, analysis of the epidemiological pattern of HAV infection, taking into account the socio-economic and sanitary conditions, geographic localisation and climate, showed that viral rate detected in West-central Tunisia is slightly higher (62.96% to 69.2%) than in East-central (50.62% to 65.7%) (Ouardani et al., 2015, 2016). Analysis of the seasonal distribution of HAV in wastewater, conducted in different parts of Tunisia, have shown that HAV circulates throughout the year with certain seasonal variation. In these studies, highest viral rates were found during summer (67.07%) in coastal areas and during winter (85.4%) and autumn (80%) in West-central regions (Ouardani et al., 2015, 2016), suggesting that geographic localisation and climate may play an important role on the seasonal variation of HAV circulation. These differences would certainly be related to the proximity of these areas to the coast and the consequent condensation of tourism population, mainly from neighbouring countries such as Algeria and Libya, but also from European Union. Quantitative data showed high HAV rates during summer (10^9 GC/L) which might suggest the occurrence of outbreaks in this period (Ouardani et al., 2015, 2016).

Phylogenetic studies of HAV conducted in Tunisia from wastewater samples showed the predominance of the sub-genotype IA over several years with the presence of some strains closely related to European strains demonstrating the circulation of this sub-genotype variant in the Mediterranean region (Chironna et al., 2003). However, the sub-genotype IB remains infrequent in the country (Gharbi-Khelifi et al., 2006; Béji-Hamza et al., 2014; Ouardani et al., 2015, 2016) and was described in the coastal regions, especially in touristic areas, with high number detected during spring and summer (Ouardani et al., 2016). These facts suggest that this sub-genotype, circulating in Europe, may be imported by travellers during Easter or summer holidays vacation.

Hepatitis E Virus

Hepatitis E virus (HEV) is the etiologic agent of enterically transmitted non-A, non-B hepatitis in humans worldwide (Emerson and Purcell, 2003) classified as a member of the genus *Orthohepevirus,* species *Orthohepevirus A,* within the family *Hepeviridae* (Khuroo and Khuroo, 2016; Smith et al., 2016). As for HAV only one serotype has been described for HEV but four major genotypes have been identified based on nucleotide sequencing. Genotypes 1 and 2, restricted to humans, have been found in Asia, Africa and

North America, while genotypes 3 and 4 are zoonotic and can infect both humans and animals such as domestic pigs, wild boars, and other mammals (Li et al., 2005; Feagins et al., 2008). The genotype 3 is frequently found in the world whereas the genotype 4 has been found only in Asia. HEV is a positive single-stranded RNA nonenveloped virus. The genome is approximately 7.2 kb in length containing short 5' and 3' noncoding regions (UTR) and three open reading frames (ORFs 1, 2 and 3) (Wang et al., 2000; Huang et al., 2007). The virus is resistant to high temperatures at 56°C for 1 h but it is sensible to boiling, frying and chlorination (Emerson et al., 2005; Khuroo and Khuroo, 2016). HEV is primarily transmitted by the fecal-oral route (Emerson and Purcell, 2003; Phan et al., 2005) and epidemics are usually linked to contaminated water, occurring only in developing countries of Asia, Africa and in Mexico (Meng, 2010). In these countries, outbreaks of HEV infections are closely linked to poor hygienic conditions and consumption of uncontrolled water (Masclaux et al., 2013; Garcia et al., 2014).

In Tunisia, very few studies were conducted on HEV in wastewater and its prevalence remains not well known. Unlike high prevalence reported in other North African countries (Kamal et al., 2010) as well as some developing areas, where levels in wastewater reached 40.7% in Pakistan (Ahmad et al., 2010) and 55.6% in India (Vivek et al., 2013), HEV seems to be infrequent in our country with viral contamination of 2% in wastewater (Béji-Hamza et al., 2015). This result is in line with seroprevalence studies that showed low rates (4.3% - 6.8%) of HEV in Tunisian population (healthy invidious and blood donors) (Rezig et al., 2008; Houcine et al., 2012; Ben-Ayed et al., 2015). Phylogenetic analysis, conducted by Béji-Hamza and co-workers, showed the presence of genotypes 1 and 3 in environmental samples, suggesting the circulation of these two genotypes in the Tunisian population (Béji-Hamza et al., 2015).

Norovirus

Norovirus (NoV) represents the most important cause of infectious human gastroenteritis (Patel et al., 2009) and food-borne outbreaks of acute gastroenteritis worldwide (Green, 2007; Patel et al., 2008, 2009). It is a non-enveloped icosahedral virus with positive single-stranded RNA of 7.5-7.7 kb. NoVs are classified within the family *Caliciviridae*, and subdivided into five genogroups (GI–GV) (Karst et al., 2003; Zheng et al., 2006) and several serotypes. Genogroups I, II and rarely IV are known to infect humans (Green et al., 1994; Wang et al., 1994; Ando et al., 2000; Zheng et al., 2006; Patel et al., 2009) whereas GIII affects swine. Based on VP1 coding sequence analysis, more than 33 different genotypes were described within NoVs genogroups (Zheng et al., 2006; Zheng et al., 2010), with genotype II.4 being the most common cause of gastroenteritis outbreaks (Siebenga et al., 2009; Zheng et al., 2010).

Little is known about NoV occurrence in wastewater in Tunisia, and the only two studies found in the literature were carried out in the coastal region of Monastir using small samples number. Data showed a variation on the prevalence of this virus from 4.4% to 67.6% (Hassine et al., 2010; Sdiri-Loulizi et al., 2010; Hassine-Zaafrane et al., 2014), being detected during winter and spring with high rates in the months of February and May (Hassine et al., 2010). These results are one line with other reports described by Melnick (1991) and Lopman et al. (2004), demonstrating a seasonal pattern of NoV during the cold season with occasional appearance of epidemics observed especially during spring. Phylogenetic studies showed high frequency of GI NoV in the environment (Hassine-Zaafrane et al., 2014; Hmaied et al., 2015) contrary to clinical samples where GII were predominant (Hassine-Zaafrane et al. 2013). No clear explanation for this discrepancy was found but authors suggested the possibility of infection by various genotypes of NoV with GI strains might be more resistant in wastewater and less severe or lead to asymptomatic infections compared to GII (Duizer et al., 2004; Rzeżutka and Cook, 2004; da Silva et al., 2007).

ROTAVIRUS

Rotavirus (RV) is the principal cause of severe diarrhea in children below 5 years of age, with approximatively 140 million cases and 453,000 deaths described in developing countries each year (Steele et al., 2003; Tate et al., 2012). Group A rotavirus (RV-A) is associated with a large majority of severe gastroenteritis, in both humans and animals, occurring in developed and developing countries and represents the major cause of child mortality (Parashar et al., 2006; Sanchez-Padilla et al., 2009). RV-A is a nonenveloped icosahedral virus of 70 nm in diameter, containing 11 segments of a double-stranded RNA genome of approximately 18.5 kb (Okoh et al., 2010; Rodríguez-Lázaro et al., 2012). It is classified within *Reoviridae* family, genus *Rotavirus*, and divided into G and P genotypes. At least 27 G types and 37 P types of RV-A have been identified to date (Matthijnssens et al., 2011; Trojnar et al., 2013), of which G1-G4, G9, G12, P4 and P8 are most commonly found infecting humans (Gentsch et al., 1996; Martella et al., 2010).

Like the other enteric viruses, RV persist in the water environment (Hurst and Gerba, 1980) and its inactivation in different types of water was correlated with higher temperatures (John and Rose, 2005). Prevalence of RV-A in wastewater were determined in only some region of the East-Central Tunisia, being detected in 72.4% of wastewater samples with viral rates of 76.1% and 68.7% in raw and treated wastewater, respectively. However, variation on RV-A prevalence between STPs (from 70.8% to 81.4%) was associated to the origin of influents where domestic wastewater may contain greater quantities of virus than industrial water (Hassine-Zaafrane et al., 2015). Seasonality of RV-A was also studied and showed high prevalence during winter (28.5%) and spring (32.8%). In addition, high viral loads were observed in December, March and July which corresponded to school holidays when high influx of invidious from other regions were noted (Hellmér et al. 2014; Hassine-Zaafrane et al., 2015).

Molecular genotyping of RV-A wastewater samples in Tunisia showed a great diversity of genotypes with the presence of 10 G types and 8 P types (Hassine-Zaafrane et al., 2015). Most of them belonged to G1-G4, G9, P[4], P[6], P[8] and P[9] and described as being epidemiologically relevant for humans, while some detected genotypes as G6, G8, G10, P[1], P[5], P[11] and G5, G11, P[7] have been commonly found in bovine and swine, respectively (Papp et al. 2013; Hassine-Zaafrane et al., 2015).

Enteroviruses

Enteroviruses (Evs) are the viruses most commonly encountered in humans and infections by these viruses have been estimated at 1 billion worldwide (Palacios and Oberste, 2005). EV consists of spherical nonenveloped virus, with a positive single stranded RNA genome of 7.2–8.5 kb, belonged to the genus *Enterovirus* within the family *Picornaviridae* (Stanway et al., 2005). Actually, more than 100 serotypes of enteroviruses, ratified by the Executive Committee of the International Committee on Taxonomy of Viruses (ICTV) (Lauber and Gorbalenya, 2012; Adams et al., 2013), are distributed in four species in humans (A, B, C and D): EV-A contains some coxsackievirus A strains; EV-B includes coxsackievirus A9, coxsackievirus B1-6 and most of the echoviruses; EV-C comprises polioviruses 1–3 and some coxsackievirus A strains (Stanway et al., 2005).

EV68 and EV70 are the two serotypes found in the EV-D species (Smura et al., 2007). EVs can replicate in the respiratory tract and the gut and are transmitted by respiratory or faecal–oral route (Rodríguez-Lázaro et al., 2012). Although most of infections are asymptomatic, EVs can be responsible for a wide spectrum of diseases in humans, including acute paralytic poliomyelitis, aseptic meningitis, encephalitis, myocarditis, pericarditis and conjunctivitis. They are also involved in respiratory system infections and gastroenteritis as well as insulin-dependent diabetes (Wagenknecht et al., 1991; Kocwa-Haluch, 2001; Griffin et al., 2003).

EVs are highly resistant in several environments and able to preserve their infectivity for months (Wetz et al., 2004; Fong and Lipp, 2005; Rajtar et al., 2008), which reflects their widespread occurrence in populations (Sellwood et al., 1981; Hovi et al., 1996; Sedmark et al., 2003). As other enteric viruses, they can contaminate soil, food crops and natural watercourses through the discharge of contaminated wastewater. In Tunisia, the presence of EV in wastewater was also documented and most studies showed high prevalence from 30.2% to 50% (Sdiri et al., 2006; Hassine et al., 2010; Ibrahim et al., 2014). Hassine and co-workers (2010) showed, through monitoring of EVs seasonality in wastewater, a regular circulation of these viruses throughout the year (except in the months of November, February and March) with predominance during summer and autumn. It has been described that in the Mediterranean climate, EVs are endemic with possibility of outbreaks appearance during summer-autumn (Nairn and Clements, 1999; Belghuith et al., 2004). Furthermore, molecular characterization of EVs from wastewater samples has shown the circulation of the three species A, B and C in the country (Ibrahim et al., 2014).

AICHI VIRUS

Aichi virus (AiV) is a causative agent of gastroenteritis in humans, transmitted like all enteric viruses by faecal-oral route (Ambert-Balay et al., 2008). It is classified as a member of the Aichivirus species, genus *Kobuvirus* within the family *Picornaviridae* (Knowles et al. 2012). The virus is nonenveloped with an icosahedral nucleocapsid of 30 nm in diameter which protects a positive single-stranded RNA of approximately 8.3 kb in length coding for a single open reading frame (ORF) (Burutarán et al., 2016). Based on their nucleotide sequences similarity (Yamashita et al., 2000; Yamashita and Sakae, 2003; Ambert-Balay et al., 2008), AiV was divided into three genetically distinct genotypes, where genotypes A and B are more frequent than the genotype C (Ambert-Balay et al., 2008; Kaikkonen et al., 2010; Jonsson et al., 2012). Since its first identification in 1989 in Japan (Yamashita et al., 1991), AiV was isolated is several countries of Asia (Pham et al., 2007), Europe (Oh et al., 2006; Ambert-Balay et al., 2008), South America (Oh et al., 2006), at low prevalence from children suffering from gastroenteritis. To date, there are only two reports that described the occurrence of AiV in Tunisia, and showed higher viral rate of 4.1% in stool samples isolated from children (Sdiri-Loulizi et al., 2009), compared to other countries such as France (0.9%), and 6% in wastewater samples collected from several STPs located in the East-Central of the country. These results confirm that AiV present in wastewater may reflect virus circulation in the community and suggest that it is an emergent virus implicated in gastroenteritis. Moreover, it has been reported that genotype A of AiV was predominant in Tunisia, in both clinical and environmental samples, as well as in Europe and Asia (Oh et al., 2006; Ambert-Balay et al., 2008, Yamashita et al., 2000). Indeed, phylogenetic analysis showed that nucleotide sequences of the environmental strains were closely related to those found in clinical samples, suggesting a parallel evolution of the environmental and clinical strains over time.

Evaluation of Biological Wastewater Treatment Processes Used in Tunisian STPs

Waterborne transmission represents one of principal modes of indirect transmission of enteric viruses to humans and is the origin of many epidemics in developing countries (Ali et al., 2004; Bosch et al., 2005). Thus, great resistance of these viruses in water environment, inadequate wastewater treatment processes and reuse constitute a potential risk on public health since they are shed in high quantities in the faeces and subsequently can contaminate fresh products such as vegetables, salads, fruits and filter-feeding molluscs (Okoh et al., 2010; Bosch et al., 2009). These latter are able to concentrate viruses by filtration, through their gills, of large quantities of sea water (100 to 650 liters/ hour/kg of mussels) and their consumption, even raw or lightly cooked, presents a high risk of enteric virus carriage (Croci et al. 2007; Gabrieli et al. 2007).

Therefore, since wastewater represents the main source of enteric viruses (Rodríguez-Lázaro et al., 2012), the effectiveness of processes used to the treatment for viral removal should be assessed before wastewater reuse in irrigation and other sectors or release in the nature (Hmaied et al., 2015). There has been increasing concern about the evaluation of wastewater treatment processes efficiency to avoid viral environmental contamination and to develop new strategies to remove viruses. However, several studies were conducted in this field and showed an inefficiency of most of the current wastewater treatment processes to remove viruses with reduction rates vary from 20 to 80% (Payment et al., 1986; La Rosa et al., 2010; Prado et al., 2011; Ouardani et al., 2015). Therefore, as released viruses are able to preserve their infectivity for a long period, they can easily contaminate diverse food items (Masclaux et al., 2013) and environmental waters such as lakes, rivers, sea, and drinking water resources.

As described previously, Tunisia is one of many developing countries that developed its secondary sewage treatment plants (Melhem et al., 2014) in order to reuse treated wastewater in several sectors, mainly in agriculture, to palliate the lack of water resources (Jebri et al., 2012). It has been reported that the government is investigating the reuse of these waters to refill the aquifers, forests irrigation and in industry through pilot projects. However, quality of treated wastewater remains poor (El Ayni et al., 2013) and the lack of specific surveillance program for enteric viruses in wastewaters (Sdiri-Loulizi et al., 2010) could, among many risk factors (Jacobsen and Koopman, 2005; Rodríguez-Lázaro et al., 2012; Melhem et al., 2014; La Rosa et al., 2014), increase public health risk related to the viral contamination in wastewater. Indeed, given that Tunisia is ranked between countries highly endemic for almost enteric viruses causing hepatitis and gastroenteritis, transmission of infections may be facilitated with poor hygiene conditions and inappropriate wastewater reuse.

Little is known about the efficiency of wastewater treatment processes currently used in Tunisia to remove enteric viruses. Therefore, in several studies viruses have been detected in treated wastewater and it has been confirmed that whatever the method used by STP, it is impossible to provide virus-free wastewater (Hassine-Zaafrane et al., 2014; Hmaied et al., 2015; Ouardani et al., 2015, 2016). Tunisian urban wastewater is a mixture of human sewage, suspended solids, debris and a variety of chemical substances that originate from residential, commercial and industrial activities (Okoh et al., 2010). To ensure the depuration of these waters, STPs are using both primary and secondary treatment processes where a range of wastewater treatment options is used and treatment level varies between urban and rural areas (Qadir et al., 2010). Unfortunately, due to the rapid increase in urban population and high use of water during summer, some STPs do not have the capacity to process large volumes of wastewater and consequently retention times for wastewater treatment become too short to be effective.

Based on data provided by ONAS, the majority of Tunisian STPs are using to the depuration of urban wastewater biological secondary treatments, of which activated sludge and lagoon are the most widespread in the country (Qadir et al., 2010; Melhem et al., 2014; Ouardani et al., 2015). Within activated sludge process, we distinguish three methods as follow: conventional activated sludge (medium charge) used for large community, extended aeration activated sludge (low charge) and extended aeration oxidation ditch activated sludge (low charge) used for medium to small community. However, two varieties of lagoon processes exist, natural/ facultative lagoon and aerated lagoon, and they are used only for the treatment of small volume of wastewater. Currently, Tunisian efforts are focused on the upgrade to tertiary level treatment (Melhem et al., 2014). All these processes lead to remove pollutants, both chemical and biological, from wastewater before discharge to the environment and althought they are not intended to eliminate viruses, the effectiveness of viral reduction would probaly be improved (DeBusk, 1999; Okoh et al., 2010).

Data on the prevalence of enteric viruses in treated wastewater in Tunisia were provided in several reports and showed low viral reduction. For HAV, regardless the wastewater treatment process, removal rate reached 39.1% (Ouardani et al., 2016) which corresponded to viral reduction found in other reports (20-80%) (Payment et al., 1986; La Rosa et al., 2010; Prado et al., 2011; Ouardani et al., 2015). indeed, values in outflows (22.7%-40.7%) were slightly lower than in inflows (56.8%-66.9%). High viral concentration were also noted in treated wastewater samples collected from many STPs and ranged from 3.9 x 10^3 to 1.4 x 10^8 GC/L (Ouardani et al., 2015, 2016). Activated sludge process is widely used by cities and communities where large volumes of sewage should be treated in a cost-saving manner. The comparison of the three activated sludge processes showed a complete failure of conventional activated sludge (medium charge) with 63.6% of positive samples being detected in treated wastewater samples and viral reduction rate of 7.9% (Ouardani et al., 2016). Extended aeration and oxidation ditch activated sludge processes (low charge), used to overcome some of limitations associated with the conventional activated sludge (Benjes, 1976), had high/moderate efficiency against HAV varying from 32.4% to 91.47% (Ouardani et al., 2015, 2016). However, lagoon process seems to be better to remove HAV since Ouardani and co-workers showed a removal rates of

71.8% to 100% and viral load reduction was more than 1 log unit (Ouardani et al., 2015).

Other studies focused on molecular detection of NoV in effluents, treated by conventional activated sludge process, showing viral rates of 47.9% (Hassine-Zaafrane et al., 2014). NoV GI (83.3%-96.4%) was more prevalent than NoV GII (2%-66.6%) with viral concentrations ranged from 2.72 x 10^2 to 2.6 x 10^3 GC/L for GI and from 33 to175 GC/L for GII (Hassine-Zaafrane et al., 2014; Hmaied et al., 2015). Furthermore, RV was detected in 68.7% (Hassine-Zaafrane et al., 2015) of treated wastewater samples with high concentrations ranged from 5.2 x 10^5 to 1.3 x 10^7 GC/L (Hassine-Zaafrane et al., 2015; Hmaied et al., 2015).

These findings demonstrate the high resistance of these viruses to all kind of wastewater treatments and point to a potential health risk if final effluents are discharged into fresh or marine water systems or reused in irrigation. This low efficiency to eliminate viruses depends generally on origin of influents, viral type, wastewater pH, the nature of the suspended solid (Arraj et al., 2005), environmental conditions and wastewater treatment level (Hmaied et al., 2015). Otherwise, it has been reported that several factors may affect the efficiency and the reliability of the treatment process, such as hydraulic and organic overloads of the STP, equipment and structures very old and deteriorated, lack of operating staff and the entering of industrial wastewaters (Ouardani et al., 2016). According to a study, conducted in a variety of STPs and introducing the latter parameter on the evaluation of treatment efficiency, has shown lowest virus removal rate in STPs collecting large volume of industrial wastewaters with higher viral loads in treated wastewater than those found in raw sewage. These findings were partially explained by the fact that industrial raw wastewater contains high loads of both organic and chemical pollutants as well as heavy metals that may inhibit the PCR (Sobsey and Hickey, 1985; Tsai and Olson, 1992).

CONCLUSION

The study and assessment of enteric viruses in Tunisian wastewaters may provide an insight on viral circulation in general population, their resistance to wastewater treatment processes and to estimate the public health risks associated with these viruses. Moreover, evaluation of secondary biological wastewater treatment processes commonly used in Tunisia has important implications on the development of official controls and the establishment of viral indicators, in order to improve the microbiological control of treated wastewater, especially that this renewable source is reused for many activities, mainly in agriculture. As an example, investigations performed up to now indicate that the replacement of conventional activated sludge treatments and the establishment of tertiary treatments seems to be necessary to reduce as much as possible viral contamination of the environment.

These measures together with an improvement of hygienic practices through educational programs would be of great help to reduce and/or avoid public health problems related with enteric viruses in Tunisia.

REFERENCES

Adams, M. J., King, A. M. Q. and Carstens, E. B. (2013). Ratification vote on taxonomic proposals to the International Committee on Taxonomy of Viruses (2013). *Arch. Virol.*, *158*, 2023-2030.

Ahmad, T., Waheed, Y., Tahir, S., Safi, S. Z., Fatima, K., Afzal, M. S., Farooqi, Z. U. and Qadri, I. (2010). Frequency of HEV contamination in sewerage waters in Pakistan. *J. Infect. Dev. Ctries.*, *4*, 842-845.

Ali, M. A., Al-Herrawy, A. Z. and El-Hawaary, S. E. (2004). Detection of enteric viruses, Giardia and Cryptosporidium in two different types of drinking water treatment facilities. *Water. Res.*, *38*, 3931-3939.

Allan, J. A., (2001). The Middle East water question: hydropolitics and the global economy. London: Tauris and Co. Ltd.

Ambert-Balay, K., Lorrot, M., Bon, F., Giraudon, H., Kaplon, J., Wolfer, M., Lebon, P., Gendrel, D. and Pothier, P. (2008). Prevalence and genetic diversity of Aichi virus strains in stool samples from community and hospitalized patients. *J. Clin. Microbiol.*, *46*, 1252-1258.

Ando, T., Noel, J. S. and Fankhauser, R. L. (2000). Genetic classification of "Norwalk-like viruses". *J. Infect. Dis.* *181*, 336-348.

Arraj, A., Bohatier, J., Laveran, H. and Traore, O. (2005). Comparison of bacteriophage and enteric virus removal in pilot scale activated sludge plants. *J. Appl. Microbiol.*, *98*, 516-524.

Bahri, A. and Brissaud, F. (1996). Wastewater reuse in Tunisia: assessing a national policy. *Water. Sci. Technol.*, *33*, 87-94.

Bahri, A. (2008). Water reuse in Middle Eastern and North African countries. In Water reuse: an international survey of current practice, issues and needs, edited by B. Jimenez and T. Asano. London: IWA, 27-47.

Béji-Hamza, A., Khélifi-Gharbi, H., Hassine-Zaafrane, M., Della Libera, S., Iaconelli, M., Muscillo, M., Petricca, S., Ciccaglione, A. R., Bruni, R., Taffon, S., Equestre, M., Aouni, M. and La Rosa, G. (2014). Qualitative and Quantitative Assessment of Hepatitis A Virus in Wastewaters in Tunisia. *Food. Environ. Virol.*, *6*, 246-252.

Béji-Hamza, A., Hassine-Zaafrane, M., Khélifi-Gharbi, H., Della Libera, S., Iaconelli, M., Muscillo, M., Petricca, S., Ciccaglione, A. R., Bruni, R., Taffon, S., Aouni, M. and La Rosa, G. (2015). Hepatitis E virus genotypes 1 and 3 in wastewater samples in Tunisia. *Arch. Virol.*, *160*, 183-189.

Belguith, K., Hassen, A., Gharbi, J. and Aouni, M. (2004). Dominance de la circulation des echovirus dans les eaux usées de la région de Monastir. *Microbiol. Hyg. Alim.*, *47*, 49-53.

Ben-Ayed, Y., Hannachi, H., Ben-Alaya-Bouafif, N., Gouider, E., Triki, H. and Bahri, O. (2015). Hepatitis E virus seroprevalence among hemodialysis and hemophiliac patients in Tunisia (North Africa). *J. Med. Virol.*, *87*, 441-445.

Benjes, Jr., H. H. (1976). Small Community Wastewater Treatment Facilities - Biological Treatment Systems. Washington DC: United States Environmental Protection Agency (EPA).

Bosch, A., Abad, X. and Pintó, R. M. (2005). Human pathogenic viruses in the marine environment. In Oceans and Health: Pathogens in the Marine Environment, edited by S. Belkin and R. R. Colwell. New York: Springer, 109-131.

Bosch, A., Guix, S., Sano, D. and Pinto, R. M. (2008). New tools for the study and direct surveillance of viral pathogens in water. *Curr. Opin. Biotechnol.*, *19*, 295-301.

Bosch, A., Pinto, R. M. and Le Guyader, F. S. (2009). Viral contaminants of molluscan shellfish: detection and characterisation. In Shellfish safety and quality, edited by S. E. Shumway and G. E. Rodrick. Woodhead Publishing Series in Food Science, Technology and Nutrition No. 167.

Burutarán, L., Lizasoain, A., García, M., Tort, L. F., Colina, R. and Victoria, M. (2016). Detection and Molecular Characterization of Aichivirus 1 in Wastewater Samples from Uruguay. *Food. Environ. Virol.*, *8*, 13-17.

Byun, K. S., Kim, J. H., Song, K. J., Baek, L. J., Song, J. W., Park, S. H., Kwon, O. S., Yeon, J. E., Kim, J. S., Bak, Y. T. and Lee, C. H. (2001). Molecular epidemiology of hepatitis A in Korea. *J. Gastroenterol. Hepatol.*, *16*, 519-524.

Chironna, M., Grottola, A., Lanave, C., Villa, E., Barbuti, S. and Quarto, M. (2003). Genetic analysis of HAV strains recovered from patients with acute hepatitis from Southern Italy. *J. Med. Virol.*, *70*, 343-349.

Costafreda, M. I., Bosch, A. and Pintó, R. M. (2006). Development, evaluation, and standardization of a real-time TaqMan reverse transcription-PCR assay for quantification of hepatitis A virus in clinical and shellfish samples. *Appl. Environ. Microbiol.*, *72*, 3846-3855.

Costa-Mattioli, M., Cristina, J., Romero, H., Perez-Bercof, R., Casane, D., Colina, R., Garcia, L., Vega, I., Glikman, G., Romanowsky, V., Castello, A., Nicand, E., Gassin, M., Billaudel, S. and Ferré, V. (2002). Molecular evolution of hepatitis a virus: a new classification based on the complete VP1 protein. *J. Virol.*, *76*, 9516-9525.

Crance, J. M., Gantzer, C., Schwartzbrod, L. and Deloince, R. (1998). Effect of temperature on the survival of hepatitis A virus and its capsidal antigen in synthetic seawater. *Env. Tox. Water. Quality.*, *13*, 89-92.

Cristina, J. and Costa-Mattioli, M. (2007). Genetic variability and molecular evolution of hepatitis A virus. *Virus. Res.*, *127*, 151-157.

Croci, L., Losio, M. N., Suffredini, E., Pavoni, E., Di Pasquale, S., Fallacara, F. and Arcangeli, G. (2007). Assessment of human enteric viruses in shellfish from the northern Adriatic sea. *Int. J. Food. Microbiol.*, *114*, 252-257.

Da Silva, A. K., Le Saux, J. C., Parnaudeau, S., Pommepuy, M., Eimelech, M. and Le Guyader, F. S. (2007). Evaluation of removal of norovirus during wastewater treatment, using real-time reverse transcription-PCR: Different behaviors of genogroups I and II. *Appl. Environ. Microbiol.*, *73*, 7891-7897.

Debord, T. and Buisson, Y. (1998). Viral hepatitis of enteric origin. *Bull. Soc. Pathol. Exot.*, *91*, 428-431.

DeBusk, W. F. (1999). Wastewater treatment wetlands: contaminant removal processes. Gainesville, FL: University of Florida, IFAS Extension, 1-5.

Duizer, E., Bijkerk, P., Rockx, B., De Groot, A., Twisk, F. and Koopmans, M. (2004). Inactivation of caliciviruses. *Appl. Environ. Microbiol.*, *70*, 4538-4543.

El Ayni, F., Manoli, E., Cherif, S., Jrad, A., Assimacopoulos, D. and Trabelsi-Ayadi, M. (2013). Deterioration of a Tunisian coastal aquifer due to agricultural activities and possible approaches for better water management. *Water. Environ. J.*, *27*, 348-361.

Emerson, S. U. and Purcell, R. H. (2003). Hepatitis E virus. *Rev. Med. Virol.*, *13*, 145-154.

Emerson, S. U., Arankalle, V. A. and Purcell, R. H. (2005). Thermal stability of hepatitis E virus. *J. Infect. Dis.*, *192*, 930-933.

Enriquez, C. E., Hurst, C. J. and Gerba, C. P. (1995). Survival of enteric adenoviruses 40 and 41 in tap, sea, and waste water. *Water. Res.*, *29*, 2548-2553.

Feagins, A. R., Opriessnig, T., Huang, Y. W., Halbur, P. G. and Meng, X. J. (2008). Cross-species infection of specific-pathogen-free pigs by a genotype 4 strain of human hepatitis E virus. *J. Med. Virol.*, *80*, 1379-1386.

Fleisher, J. M., Kay, D., Wyer, M. and Merret, H. (1996). The Enterovirus test in the assessment of recreational water associated gastroenteritis. *Water. Res.*, *30*, 2341-2346.

Fong, T. T. and Lipp, E. K. (2005). Enteric viruses of humans and animals in aquatic environments: health risks, detection, and potential water quality assessment tools. *Microbiol. Mol. Biol. Rev.*, *69*, 357-371.

Gabrieli, R., Macaluso, A., Lanni, L., Saccares, S., Di Giamberardino, F., Cencioni, B., Petrinca, A. R. and Divizia, M. (2007). Enteric viruses in molluscan shellfish. *New. Microbiol.*, *30*, 471- 475.

García, M., Fernández-Barredo, S. and Pérez-Gracia, M. T. (2014). Detection of hepatitis E virus (HEV) through the different stages of pig manure composting plants. *Microb. Biotechnol.*, *7*, 26-31.

Gentsch, J. R., Woods, P. A., Ramachandran, M., Das, B. K., Leite, J. P., Alfieri, A., Kumar, R., Bhan, M. K. and Glass, R. I. (1996). Review of G and P typing results from a global collection of rotavirus strains: implications for vaccine development. *J. Infect. Dis.*, *174* (Suppl. 1), S30-S36.

Gharbi-Khelifi, H., Ferre, V., Sdiri, K., Berthome, M., Fki, L., Harrath, R., Billaudel, S. and Aouni, M. (2006). Hepatitis A in Tunisia: phylogenetic analysis of hepatitis A virus from 2001 to 2004. *J. Virol. Methods.*, *138*, 109-116.

Gharbi-Khelifi, H., Sdiri, K., Ferre, V., Harrath, R., Berthome, M., Billaudel, S. and Aouni, M. (2007). A 1-year study of the epidemiology of hepatitis A virus in Tunisia. *Clin. Microbiol. Infect.*, *13*, 25-32.

Green, S. M., Dingle, K. E., Lambden, P. R., Caul, E. O., Ashley, C. R. and Clarke, I. N. (1994). Human enteric Caliciviridae: A new prevalent small round-structured virus group defined by RNA-dependent RNA polymerase and capsid diversity. *J. Gen. Virol.*, *75*, 1883-1888.

Green, K. Y. (2007). Caliciviridae: the noroviruses. In Fields Virology, edited by D. M. Knipe, P. M. Howley, D. E. Griffin, R. A. Lamb, M. A. Martin, B. Roizman, and S. E. Straus. Philadelphia: Lippincott-Raven Publishers, 949-979.

Griffin, D. W., Donaldson, K. A., Paul, J. H. and Rose, J. B. (2003). Pathogenic human viruses in coastal waters. *Clin. Microbiol. Rev.*, *16*, 129-143.

Hassine, M., Sdiri, K., Riabi, S., Beji, A., Aouni, Z. and Aouni, M. (2010). Detection of enteric viruses in wastewater of Monastir region by RT-PCR method. *Tunis. Med.*, *88*, 70-75.

Hassine-Zaafrane, M., Sdiri-Loulizi, K., Kaplon, J., Ben Salem, I., Pothier, P., Aouni, M. and Ambert-Balay, K. (2013). Prevalence and genetic diversity of norovirus infection in Tunisian children (2007- 2010). *J. Med. Virol.*, *85*, 1100-1110.

Hassine-Zaafrane, M., Sdiri-Loulizi, K., Kaplon, J., Ben Salem, I., Pothier, P., Aouni, M. and Ambert-Balay, K. (2014). Molecular detection of human noroviruses in influent and effluent samples from two biological sewage treatment plants in the region of Monastir, Tunisia. *Food. Environ. Virol.*, *6*, 125-131.

Hassine-Zaafrane, M., Kaplon, J., Ben Salem, I., Sdiri-Loulizi, K., Sakly, N., Pothier, P., Aouni, M. and Ambert-Balay, K. (2015). Detection and genotyping of group A rotaviruses isolated from sewage samples in Monastir, Tunisia between April 2007 and April 2010. *J. Appl. Microbiol.*, *119*, 1443-1453.

Hellmér, M., Paxéus, N., Magnius, L., Enache, L., Arnholm, B., Johansson, A., Bergström, T. and Norder, H. (2014). Detection of pathogenic viruses in sewage provided early warnings of hepatitis A virus and norovirus outbreaks. *Appl. Environ. Microbiol.*, *80*, 6771-6781.

Hmaied, F., Keskes, S., Jebri, S., Amri, I., Yahya, M., Loisy-Hamon, F., Lebeau, B. and Hamdi, M. (2015). Removal of Rotavirus and Bacteriophages by Membrane Bioreactor Technology from Sewage. *Curr. Microbiol.*, *71*, 540-545.

Hollinger, F. B. and Emerson, S. U. (2007). Hepatitis A virus. In: Fields' Virology. Knipe DM, Howley PM (Eds). Lippincott Williams and Wilkins, PA, USA, pp. 911–947.

Houcine, N., Jacques, R., Salma, F., Anne-Gaëlle, D., Amin, S., Mohsen, H., Hamadi, B., Christophe, R., Patrice, A., Mahjoub, A. and Caroline, S. (2012). Seroprevalence of hepatitis E virus infection in rural and urban populations, Tunisia. *Clin. Microbiol. Infect.*, *18*, E119-E121.

Hovi, T., Stenvik, M. and Rosenlew, M. (1996). Relative abundance of enterovirus serotypes in sewage differs from that in patients: clinical and epidemiological implications. *Epidemiol. Infect.*, *116*, 91-97.

Huang, Y. W., Opriessnig, T., Halbur, P. G. and Meng, X. J. (2007). Initiation at the third in-frame AUG codon of open reading frame 3 of the hepatitis E virus is essential for viral infectivity *in vivo*. *J. Virol.*, *81*, 3018-3026.

Hurst, C. J. and Gerba, C. P. (1980). Stability of simian rotavirus in fresh and estuarine water. *Appl. Environ. Microbiol.*, *39*, 1-5.

Ibrahim, W., Ouerdani, I., Pillet, S., Aouni, M., Pozzetto, B. and Harrath, R. (2014). Direct typing of human enteroviruses from wastewater samples. *J. Virol. Methods.*, *207*, 215-219.

INNORPI (Institut National de la Normalisation et de la Propriété Industrielle). (1989a). *Normes de rejet dans un milieu hydrique*, NT 106.02.

INNORPI (Institut National de la Normalisation et de la Propriété Industrielle). (1989b). *Normes de réutilisation des eaux traitées en Agriculture*, NT 106.03.

Jacobsen, K. H. and Koopman, J. S. (2005). The effects of socioeconomic development on worldwide hepatitis A virus seroprevalence patterns. *Int. J. Epidemiol.*, *34*, 600-609.

Jagannathan, N. V., Mohamed, A. S. and Kremer, A. (2009). Water in the Arab World: management perspectives and innovations. The World Bank, Middle East and North Africa (MNA) Region, Washington.

Jebri, S., Jofre, J., Barkallah, I., Saidi, M. and Hmaied, F. (2012). Presence and fate of coliphages and enteric viruses in three wastewater treatment plants effluents and activated sludge from Tunisia. *Environ. Sci. Pollut. Res. Int.*, *19*, 2195-2201.

John, D. E. and Rose, J. B. (2005). Review of factors affecting microbial survival in groundwater. *Environ. Sci. Technol.*, *39*, 7345-7356.

Jonsson, N., Wahlström, K., Svensson, L., Serrander, L. and Lindberg, A. M. (2012). Aichi virus infection in elderly people in Sweden. *Arch. Virol.*, *157*, 1365-1369.

Journal Officiel de la République Tunisienne. (2010). 84: 2885. http://faolex.fao.org/docs/pdf/tun107122.pdf.

Kaikkonen, S., Räsänen, S., Rämet, M. and Vesikari, T. (2010). Aichi virus infection in children with acute gastroenteritis in Finland. *Epidemiol. Infect.*, *138*, 1166-1171.

Kamal, S. M., Mahmoud, S., Hafez, T. and El-Fouly, R. (2010). Viral hepatitis A to E in South Mediterranean countries. *Mediterr. J. Hematol. Infect. Dis.*, *2*, e2010001.

Karst, S. M., Wobus, C. E., Lay, M., Davidson, J. and Virgin, H. W. (2003). STAT1-dependent innate immunity to a Norwalk-like virus. *Science.*, *299*, 1575-1578.

Khuroo, M. S. and Khuroo, M. S. (2016). Hepatitis E: an emerging global disease - from discovery towards control and cure. *J. Viral. Hepat.*, *23*, 68-79.

Knowles, N. J., Hovi, T., Hyypia, T., King, A. M. Q., Lindberg, A. M., Pallansch, M. A., et al. (2012). Picornaviridae. In Virus taxonomy: classification and nomenclature of viruses: ninth report of the international committee on taxonomy of viruses, edited by A. M. Q. King, M. J. Adams, E. B. Carstens, and E. J. Lefkowitz. San Diego: Elsevier, 855-880.

Kocwa-Haluch, R. (2001). Waterborne enteroviruses as a hazard for human health. *Polish. J. Environ. Studies.*, *10*, 485-487.

Koopmans, M. and Duizer, E. (2004). Foodborne viruses: an emerging problem. *Int. J. Food. Microbiol.*, *90*, 23-41.

Kukkula, M., Arstila, P., Klossner, M. L., Maunula, L., Bonsdorff, C. H. and Jaatinen, P. (1997). Waterborne outbreak of viral gastroenteritis. *Scand. J. Infect. Dis.*, *29*, 415-418.

La Rosa, G., Pourshaban, M., Iaconelli, M. and Muscillo, M. (2010). Quantitative real-time PCR of enteric viruses in influent and effluent samples from wastewater treatment plants in Italy. *Ann. Ist. Super. Sanità.*, *46*, 266-273.

La Rosa, G., Libera, S. D., Iaconelli, M., Ciccaglione, A. R., Bruni, R., Taffon, S., Equestre, M., Alfonsi, V., Rizzo, C., Tosti, M. E., Chironna, M., Romanò, L., Zanetti, A. R. and Muscillo, M. (2014). Surveillance of hepatitis A virus in urban sewages and comparison with cases notified in the course of an outbreak, Italy 2013. *BMC. Infect. Dis.*, *14*, 419.

Lauber, C. and Gorbalenya, A. E. (2012). Toward genetics-based virus taxonomy: comparative analysis of a genetics-based classification and the taxonomy of picornaviruses. *J. Virol.*, *86*, 3905-3915.

Letaief, A., Kaabia, N., Gaha, R., Bousaadia, A., Lazrag, F., Trabelsi, H., Ghannem, H. and Letaief, J. (2005). Age-specific seroprevalence of hepatitis A among school children in central Tunisia. *Am. J. Trop. Med. Hyg.*, *73*, 40-43.

Li, T. C., Chijiwa, K., Sera, N., Ishibashi, T., Etoh, Y., Shinohara, Y., Kurata, Y., Ishida, M., Sakamoto, S., Takeda, N. and Miyamura, T. (2005). Hepatitis E virus transmission from wild boar meat. *Emerg. Infect. Dis.*, *11*, 1958-1960.

Lopman, B., Vennema, H., Kohli, E., Pothier, P., Sanchez, A., Negredo, A., Buesa, J., Schreier, E., Reacher, M. and Brown, D. (2004). Increase in viral gastroenteritis outbreaks in Europe and epidemic spread of new norovirus variant. *The Lancet.*, *363*, 682-688.

Lu, L., Ching, K. Z., de Paula, V. S., Nakano, T., Siegl, G., Weitz, M. and Robertson, B. H. (2004). Characterization of the complete genomic sequence of genotype II hepatitis A virus (CF53/Berne isolate). *J. Gen. Virol.*, *85*, 2943-2952.

Martella, V., Banyai, K., Matthijnssens, J., Buonavoglia, C. and Ciarlet, M. (2010). Zoonotic aspects of rotaviruses. *Vet. Microbiol.*, *140*, 246-255.

Masclaux, F. G., Hotz, P., Friedli, D., Savova-Bianchi, D. and Oppliger, A. (2013). High occurrence of hepatitis E virus in samples from wastewater treatment plants in Switzerland and comparison with other enteric viruses. *Water. Res.*, *47*, 5101-5109.

Matthijnssens, J., Ciarlet, M., McDonald, S. M., Attoui, H., Banyai, K., Brister, J. R., Buesa, J., Esona, M. D., Estes, M. K., Gentsch, J. R., Iturriza-Gómara, M., Johne, R., Kirkwood, C. D., Martella, V., Mertens, P. P., Nakagomi, O., Parreño, V., Rahman, M., Ruggeri, F. M., Saif, L. J., Santos, N., Steyer, A., Taniguchi, K., Patton, J. T., Desselberger, U. and Van Ranst, M. (2011). Uniformity of rotavirus strain nomenclature proposed by the Rotavirus Classification Working Group (RCWG). *Arch. Virol.*, *156*, 1397-1413.

Melhem, N. M., Talhouk, R., Rachidi, H. and Ramia, S. (2014). Hepatitis A virus in the Middle East and North Africa region: a new challenge. *J. Viral. Hepat.*, *21*, 605-615.

Melnick, J. L. (1991). Enteroviruses. In: Viral infections of humans. Epidemiology and control, 3rd Edition, edited by S. E. Evans. New York: Plenum Publishing corp., 191-263.

Meng, X. J. (2010). Hepatitis E virus: animal reservoirs and zoonotic risk. *Vet. Microbiol.*, *140*, 256-265.

Ministère de l'Agriculture de Tunisie. Stratégie du secteur de l'eau en Tunisie à long terme (2030). EAU XXI. Tunis: ministère de l'Agriculture, 1998.

Nainan, O. V., Margolis, H. S., Robertson, B. H., Balayan, M. and Brinton, M. A. (1991). Secuence analysis of a new Hepatitis A Virus naturally infecting Cynomolgus macaques (Macaca fascicularis). *J. Gen. Virol.*, *72*, 1685- 1689.

Nairn, C. and Clements, G. B. (1999). A study of enterovirus isolation in Glasgow from 1977 to 1997. *J. Med. Virol.*, *58*, 304-312.

Neubert, S. and Benabdallah, S. (2003). *La réutilisation des eaux usées traitées en Tunisie*. Etudes et rapports d'expertise 11/2003.

Oh, D. Y., Silva, P. A., Hauroeder, B., Diedrich, S., Cardoso, D. D. and Schreier, E. (2006). Molecular characterization of the first Aichi viruses isolated in Europe and in South America. *Arch. Virol.*, *151*, 1199-1206.

Okoh, A. I., Sibanda T. and Gusha, S. S. (2010). Inadequately Treated Wastewater as a Source of Human Enteric Viruses in the Environment. *Int. J. Environ. Res. Public. Health.*, *7*, 2620-2637.

Ouardani, I., Manso, C. F., Aouni, M. and Romalde, J. L. (2015). Efficiency of hepatitis A virus removal in six sewage treatment plants from central Tunisia. *Appl. Microbiol. Biotechnol.*, *99*, 10759-10769.

Ouardani, I., Turki, S., Aouni, M. and Romalde, J. L. (2016). Detection and Molecular Characterization of Hepatitis A Virus from Tunisian Wastewater Treatment Plants with Different Secondary Treatments. *Appl. Environ. Microbiol.*, *82*, 3834-3845.

Palacios, G. and Oberste, M. S. (2005). Enteroviruses as agents of emerging infectious diseases. *J. Neurovirol.*, *11*, 424-433.

Papp, H., Laszlo, B., Jakab, F., Ganesh, B., De Grazia, S., Matthijenssens, J., Ciarlet, M., Martella, V. and Bányai, K. (2013). Review of group A rotavirus strains reported in swine and cattle. *Vet. Microbiol.*, *165*, 190-199.

Parashar, U. D., Gibson, C. J., Bresse, J. S. and Glass, R. I. (2006). Rotavirus and severe childhood diarrhea. *Emerg. Infect. Dis.*, *12*, 304-306.

Patel, M. M., Widdowson, M. A., Glass, R. I., Akazawa, K., Vinje, J., Parashar, U. D., (2008). Systematic literature review of role of noroviruses in sporadic gastroenteritis. *Emerg. Infect. Dis.*, *14*, 1224-1231.

Patel, M. M., Hall, A. J., Vinje, J., Parashar, U. D. (2009). Noroviruses: a comprehensive review. *J. Clin. Virol.*, *44*, 1-8.

Payment, P., Fortin, S. and Trudel, M. (1986). Elimination of human enteric viruses during conventional wastewater treatment by activated sludge. *Can. J. Microbiol.*, *32*, 922-925.

Pérez-Sautu, U., Costafreda, M. I., Cayla, J., Caylà, J., Tortajada, C., Lite, J., Bosch, A. and Pintó, R. M. (2011). Hepatitis A virus vaccine escape variants and potential new serotype emergence. *Emerg. Infect. Dis.*, *17*, 734-738.

Pham, N. T., Khamrin, P., Nguyen, T. A., Kanti, D. S., Phan, T. G., Okitsu, S. and Ushijima, H. (2007). Isolation and molecular characterization of Aichi viruses from fecal specimens collected in Japan, Bangladesh, Thailand, and Vietnam. *J. Clin. Microbiol.*, *45*, 2287-2288.

Phan, T. G., Nguyen, T. A., Yan, H., Okitsu, S. and Ushijima, H. (2005). A novel RT-multiplex PCR for enteroviruses, hepatitis A and E viruses and influenza A virus among infants and children with diarrhea in Vietnam. *Arch. Virol.*, *150*, 1175-1185.

Pintó, R. M., Costafreda, M. I. and Bosch, A. (2009). Risk assessment in shellfish-borne outbreaks of hepatitis A. *Appl. Environ. Microbiol.*, *75*, 7350e7355.

Pintó, R. M., D'Andrea, L., Pérez-Rodriguez, F. J., Costafreda, M. I., Ribes, E., Guix, S. and Bosch A. (2012). Hepatitis A virus evolution and the potential emergence of new variants escaping the presently available vaccines. *Future. Microbiol.*, *7*, 331-346.

Prado, T., Silva, D. M., Guilayn, W. C., Rose, T. L., Gaspar, A. M. and Miagostovich, M. P. (2011). Quantification and molecular characterization of enteric viruses detected in effluents from two hospital wastewater treatment plants. *Water. Res.*, *45*, 1287-1297.

Qadir, M., Sharma, B. R., Bruggeman, A., Choukr-Allah, R. and Karajeh, F. (2007). Non-conventional water resources and opportunities for water augmentation to achieve food security in water scarce countries. *Agric. Water. Manag.*, *87*, 2-22.

Qadir, M., Bahri, A., Sato, T. and Al-Karadsheh, E. (2010). Wastewater production, treatment, and irrigation in Middle East and North Africa. *Irrig. Drainage. Syst.*, *24*, 37-51.

Rajtar, B., Majek, M., Polański, Ł. and Polz-Dacewicz, M. (2008). Enteroviruses in water environment--a potential threat to public health. *Ann. Agric. Environ. Med.*, *15*, 199-203.

Rezig, D., Ouneissa, R., Mhiri, L., Mejri, S., Haddad-Boubaker. S., Ben Alaya, N. and Triki, H. (2008). Seroprevalences of hepatitis A and E infections in Tunisia. *Pathol. Biol.*, *56*, 148-153.

Rodríguez-Lázaro, D., Cook, N., Ruggeri, F. M., Sellwood, J., Nasser, A., Nascimento, M. S., D'Agostino, M., Santos, R., Saiz, J. C., Rzeżutka, A., Bosch, A., Gironés, R., Carducci, A., Muscillo, M., Kovač, K., Diez-Valcarce, M., Vantarakis, A., von Bonsdorff, C. H., de Roda Husman, A. M., Hernández, M. and van der Poel, W. H. (2012). Virus hazards from food, water and other contaminated environments. *FEMS. Microbiol. Rev.*, *36*, 786-814.

Rzeżutka, A. and Cook, N. (2004). Survival of human enteric viruses in the environment and food. *FEMS. Microbiol. Rev.*, (28), 441-453.

Sanchez, G., Pinto, R. M., Vanaclocha, H. and Bosch, A. (2002). Molecular characterization of hepatitis a virus isolates from a transcontinental shellfish-borne outbreak. *J. Clin. Microbiol.*, *40*, 4148-4155.

Sánchez-Padilla, E., Grais, R. F., Guerin, P. J., Steele, A. D., Burny, M. E. and Luquero, F. J. (2009). Burden of disease and circulating serotypes of rotavirus infection in sub-Saharan Africa: systematic review and meta-analysis. *Lancet. Infect. Dis.*, *9*, 567-576.

Sdiri, K., Khelifi, H., Belghith, K. and Aouni, M. (2006). Comparison of cell culture and RT-PCR for the detection of enterovirus in sewage and shellfish. *Pathol. Biol.*, *54*, 280-284.

Sdiri-Loulizi, K., Hassine, M., Gharbi-Khelifi, H., Sakly, N., Chouchane, S., Guediche, M. N., Pothier, P., Aouni, M. and Ambert-Balay, K. (2009). Detection and genomic characterization of Aichi viruses in stool samples from children in Monastir, Tunisia. *J. Clin. Microbiol.*, *47*, 2275-2278.

Sdiri-Loulizi K., Hassine, M., Aouni, Z., Gharbi-Khelifi, H., Chouchane, S., Sakly, N., Neji-Guédiche, M., Pothier, P., Aouni, M. and Ambert-Balay K. (2010). Detection and molecular characterization of enteric viruses in environmental samples in Monastir, Tunisia between January 2003 and April 2007. *J. Appl. Microbiol.*, *109*, 1093-1104.

Sedmark, G., Bina, D. and MacDonald, J. (2003). Assessment of an enterovirus sewage surveillance system by comparison of clinical isolates with sewage from Milwaukee, Wisconsin, collected Aug 1994 to Dec 2002. *Appl. Environ. Microbiol.*, *69*, 7181-7187.

Sellwood, J., Dadswell, J. V. and Slade, J. S. (1981). Viruses in sewage as an indicator of their presence in the community. *J. Hyg. Camb.*, *86*, 217-225.

Siebenga, J. J., Vennema, H., Zheng, D. P., Vinjé, J., Lee, B. E., Pang, X. L., Ho, E. C., Lim, W., Choudekar, A., Broor, S., Halperin, T., Rasool, N. B., Hewitt, J., Greening, G. E., Jin, M., Duan, Z. J., Lucero, Y., O'Ryan, M., Hoehne, M., Schreier, E., Ratcliff, R. M., White, P. A., Iritani, N., Reuter, G. and Koopmans, M. (2009). Norovirus illness is a global problem: emergence and spread of norovirus GII.4 variants, 2001–2007. *J. Infect. Dis.*, *200*, 802-812.

Smith, D. B., Paddy, J. O. and Simmonds, P. (2016). The use of human sewage screening for community surveillance of hepatitis E virus in the UK. *J. Med. Virol.*, *88*, 915-918.

Smura, T. P., Junttila, N., Blomqvist, S., Norder, H., Kaijalainen, S., Paananen, A., Magnius, L. O., Hovi, T. and Roivainen, M. (2007). Enterovirus 94, a proposed new serotype in human enterovirus species D. *J. Gen. Virol.*, *88*, 849-858.

Sobsey, M. D. and Hickey, A. R. (1985). Effects of humic and fulvic acids on poliovirus concentration from water by microporous filtration. *Appl. Environ. Microbiol.*, *49*, 259-264.

Sobsey, M. D., Shields, P. A., Hauchman, F. H., Hazard, R. L. and Caton III, L. W. (1989). Survival and transport of hepatitis A virus in soils, groundwater and wastewater. *Water. Sci. Technol.*, *10*, 97-106.

Springthorpe, V. S., Loh, C. L., Robertson, W. J. and Sattar, S. A. (1993). *In situ* survival of indicator bacteria, MS-2 phage and human pathogenic viruses in river water. *Water. Sci. Technol.*, *27*, 413-420.

Stanway, G., Brown, F., Christian, P., et al. (2005). Picornaviridae. In Virus Taxonomy – 8th Report of the International Committee on Taxonomy Viruses, edited by C. M. Fauquet, M. A. Mayo, J. Maniloff, U. Desselberger, and L. A. Bull. London: Elsevier Academic Press, 757-778.

Steele, A. D., Peenze, I., de Beer M. C., Pager, C. T., Yeats, J., Potgieter, N., Ramsaroop, U., Page, N. A., Mitchell, J. O., Geyer, A., Bos, P. and Alexander, J. J. (2003). Anticipating rotavirus vaccines: epidemiology and surveillance of rotavirus in South Africa. *Vaccine.*, *21*, 354-360.

Tate, J. E., Burton, A. H., Boschi-Pinto, C., Steele, A. D., Duque, J. and Parashar, U. D. WHO-coordinated Global Rotavirus Surveillance Network., 2012. 2008 estimate of worldwide rotavirus- associated mortality in children younger than 5 years before the introduction of universal rotavirus vaccination programmes: a systematic review and meta-analysis. *Lancet. Infect. Dis.*, *12*, 136-141.

Trojnar, E., Sachsenroder, J., Twardziok, S., Reetz, J., Otto, P. H. and Johne, R. (2013). Identification of an avian group A rotavirus containing a novel VP4 gene with a close relationship to those of mammalian rotaviruses. *J. Gen. Virol.*, *94*, 136-142.

Tsai, Y. L. and Olson, B. H. (1992). Rapid method for separation of bacterial DNA from humic substances in sediments for polymerase chain reaction. *Appl. Environ. Microbiol.*, *58*, 2292-2295.

Tsarev, S. A., Emerson, S. U., Balayan, M. S., Ticehurts, J., Purcell, R. H., (1991). Simian Hepatitis A Virus (HAV) strain AGM-27: comparision of genome structure and growth in cell culture with other HAV strains. *J. Gen. Virol.*, *72*, 1677-1686.

Vivek, R., Zachariah, U. G., Ramachandran, J., Eapen, C. E., Rajan, D. P. and Kang, G. (2013). Characterization of hepatitis E virus from sporadic hepatitis cases and sewage samples from Vellore, south India. *Trans. R. Soc. Trop. Med. Hyg.*, *107*, 363-367.

Wagenknecht, L. E., Roseman, J. M. and Herman, W. H. (1991). Increased incidence of insulin-dependent diabetes mellitus following an epidemic of coxsackievirus B5. *Am. J. Epidemiol.*, *133*, 1024-1031.

Wang, J., Jiang, X., Madore, H. P., Gray, J., Desselberger, U., Ando, T., Seto, Y., Oishi, I., Lew, J. F. and Green, K. Y. (1994). Sequence diversity of small, round-structured viruses in the Norwalk virus group. *J. Virol.*, *68*, 5982-5990.

Wang, Y., Zhang, H., Ling, R., Li, H. and Harrison, T. J. (2000). The complete sequence of hepatitis E virus genotype 4 reveals an alternative strategy for translation of open reading frames 2 and 3. *J. Gen. Virol.*, *81*, 1675-1686.

Wetz, J. J., Lipp, E. K., Griffin, D. W., Lukasik, J., Wait, D., Sobsey, M. D., Scott, T. M. and Rose, J. B. (2004). Presence, infectivity, and stability of enteric viruses in seawater: relationship to marine water quality in the Florida Keys. *Mar. Pollut. Bull.*, *48*, 698-704.

Yamashita, T., Kobayashi, S., Sakae, K., Nakata, S., Chiba, S., Ishihara, Y. and Isomura, S. (1991). Isolation of cytopathic small round viruses with BS-C-1 cells from patients with gastroenteritis. *J. Infect. Dis.*, *164*, 954-957.

Yamashita, T., Sugiyama, M., Tsuzuki, H., Sakae, K., Suzuki, Y. and Miyazaki, Y. (2000). Application of a reverse transcription-PCR for identification and differentiation of Aichi virus, a new member of the Picornavirus family associated with gastroenteritis in humans. *J. Clin. Microbiol.*, *38*, 2955-2961.

Yamashita, T. and Sakae, K. (2003). Molecular biology and epidemiology of Aichi virus and other diarrhoeogenic enteroviruses. In Perspectives in medical virology, edited by U. Desselberger and J. Gray. Amsterdam: Elsevier, 645-657.

Zheng, D. P., Ando, T., Fankhauser, R. L., Beard, R. S., Glass, R. I. and Monroe, S. S. (2006). Norovirus classification and proposed strain nomenclature. *Virology.*, *346*, 312-323.

Zheng, D. P., Widdowson, M. A., Glass, R. I. and Vinjé, J. (2010). Molecular epidemiology of genogroup II-genotype 4 noroviruses in the United States between 1994 and 2006. *J. Clin. Microbiol.*, *48*, 168-177.

In: Tunisia
Editor: Eunice Wagner

ISBN: 978-1-53610-061-7
© 2016 Nova Science Publishers, Inc.

Chapter 7

CLIMATE CHANGE EFFECTS ON EVAPOTRANSPIRATION ESTIMATED BY DIFFERENT EMPIRICAL MODELS UNDER A MEDITERRANEAN ENVIRONMENT

Basma Latrech, Hiba Ghazouani, Amel Mguidich, Boutheina Douh Mhamdi* and Abdelhamid Boujelben
Height Agronomic Institute of Chott Meriem,
University of Sousse, Tunisia

ABSTRACT

Water scarcity is among the main problems to be faced by many societies on the World in the XXIst century. It is due the combination between the increase of urban and industrial needs and the effects of climate change. The approach to estimate climate change impacts on water resources consist on union between climate model outputs and hydrological models. However, due to the coarse resolution of Global Circulation Models (GCM), their outputs should been downscaled to match the scale of interest for an impact study. In literature, two downscaling methods have been showed. The first approach is Dynamical Downscaling (DD) and the second is Statistical Downscaling (SD) approach. Until now, the impacts of climate change on evapotranspiration

* E-mail: boutheina_douh@yahoo.fr.

have not been conclusively determined. Generally decrease in rainfall and increase in temperature will result in increase in evapotranspiration. In this context, the sustainable management of water resources requires a good control of the hydrological terms. Evapotranspiration, as the major component of water cycle, is the main way for water consumption of earth system. The accurate estimation of evapotranspiration has a great importance in hydrological modeling, irrigation planning and water resources management. In the Mediterranean regions, especially in Tunisia, the main climate is characterized by an important evaporation potential. This particularity is due to the conjugation between different climatic parameters. In Tunisia, irrigated agriculture uses about 83% of the total water resources. Thus, estimating evapotranspiration is the most important step for calculating crop water requirements that has a special economic importance in rationalization of water consumption in the agricultural field. Physically-based and empirical methods to estimate evapotranspiration are evaluated in different climatic environment under current climate conditions but also under recent, and in a changing climate.

Keywords: **c**limatic change, evapotranspiration, sustainable management, statistical downscaling, dynamical downscaling

1. INTRODUCTION

The climate system of the earth, globally and regionally, has changed from the pre-industrial period to the present (Chaouech and al., 2010). Some of the changes are due to natural phenomena and some due to human activities. The CO_2 content has increased from about 280 ppm over the last thousand years to more than 360 ppm; the methane content has more than doubled; and other gases have seen a similar exponential increase (N_2O, CFC). However, the net effect of the greenhouse gases is to warm the climate system. Additional, the aerosol loading of the atmosphere has also increased, which will deepen the problem (Le treut, 2003). Thus, global warming in the last 100 years has caused about a 0.74°C increase in global average temperature. This is up from the 0.6°C increased in the 100 years prior to the Third Assessment Report of IPCC. Also the eleven years between 1995 and 2006 are recorded within the top 12 warmest years since the instrumental recording has begun (IPCC, 2007). In this context, General Circulation Models (GCMs), are the primary source of information for assessments of the future impacts of climate change (Prudhomme and al., 2002). These GCMs have resolutions of hundreds of kilometers, whilst regional climate models (RCMs) may be as fine as tens of kilometers. However, impact assessment applications often require point specific climate projections in order to capture fine scale climate variations, particularly in regions with complex topography, coastal or island locations, and in areas of highly heterogeneous land-cover. Therefore a gap exists between what climate models can predict about future climate change and the information relevant for environmental studies. Statistical and Dynamical Downscaling Models (SDMs) are commonly used to resolve this gap (Timbal and al, 2008).

According to Ravazzani and al., (2014), climate change has significant implications for the environment water resources and human life in general, which have motivated a multitude of scientific investigations over the past two decades. One of the expected impacts of climate change is a modification of water availability, due to the strict interaction between the climate system and the hydrological cycle. Along the last decade, the direct impacts of climate change registered in the Mediterranean basin consist of lower levels of precipitations, a modification of the intensity and distribution of the precipitations, an increase in floods and a raise in temperatures (IPCC, 2007). Reference evapotranspiration (ETo) is an important balancing component of the hydrological cycle, plays a key role in estimating crop growth, water demand and irrigation water management. Changes in climatic factors also affected all elements of hydrologic cycle, such as precipitation, evapotranspiration, runoff, and groundwater flow in a variety of ways. In addition to the effects on runoff through the changes of temperature and precipitation, climate change influences evaporation to a high degree. Many studies indicated that the change of ETo in the context of climate change is based not only on temperature but also on relative humidity, solar radiation and wind speed in different regions of the world (Zhang and al., 2015). However, despite the observed increases in average temperature, observations indicated that the rate of pan evaporation has been steadily declined in most parts of the world in the past several decades. The phenomenon that the global temperature increases and ETo decreases take place simultaneously is called the pan evaporation paradox (Zhang and al., 2015). Changes in ETo are of great significance for water resource planning, irrigation requirement and agricultural production. This variable influences crop growth and soil moisture, depending on the local climatic conditions. For climate and crop changes, understanding ETo can prove useful for improving crop growth and irrigation water management.

2. Climate Change and Modeling of the Climate Evolution

2.1. Global Climate Change

The climate change phenomenon is caused by greenhouse gasses, which affect the greenhouse properties of the earth's atmosphere. Since industrialization in the 1900s, greenhouse gasses' emissions have been increased due to increasing in fossil fuel burning (Dastorani and Poormohammadi, 2012). However, over the last thousand years, the CO_2 content has increased from about 280 ppm to more than 360 ppm; the methane content has more than doubled; and other gases have seen a similar exponential increase (N_2O, CFC) (Le treut, 2003). Moreover, these gasses allow solar radiation to travel from the sun to the ground but prevent the reflected heat from the surface into the space. This causes to rise the earth's temperature, gradually (Dastorani and Poormohammadi, 2012). In fact, in the last 100 years, global warming has caused about a 0.74°C increase in global average temperature. This is up from the 0.6°C increased in the 100 years prior to the Third Assessment Report of IPCC. Also the eleven years between 1995 and 2006 are recorded within the top 12 warmest years since the instrumental recording has begun (IPCC, 2007). Therefore climate simulation models serve as useful tools for assessing possible effects of climate change. Recent developments in climate change forecast using global and regional climate models made it possible to provide more detailed information on temperature and precipitation changes.

2.2. General Circulation Models (GCMs)

General Circulation Models (GCMs), are the primary source of information for assessments of the future impacts of climate change (Prudhomme and al., 2002). However, GCMs are used to simulate climate on a global scale, typically have a horizontal resolution of 300 km. Thus, GCMs are inadequate to represent hydrological processes at scales smaller than the continental scale (Majone and al., 2012). For some types of impact assessment (risk of drought or flooding on large catchments) a really averaged quantities such as the grid box variables output from a GCM may be sufficient. In many cases, information will be required at a network of point locations implying the need to downscale the GCM output. This is particularly true when the model results are required to drive impact models such as agricultural crop models (Murphy, 1998). According to Prudhomme and al., (2002) some of the problems associated with GCMs in the early 1990s have been solved, improving significantly the reliability of modeling the climate under global warming. In this context, two GCMs' generations were developed:

- First generation of GCMs: assumed that the concentration of CO_2 equivalent gases in the atmosphere had reached equilibrium before the experiments were run. In addition, coupling between the climate modeled over the land and the ocean was hardly present, leading to potential differences in land cells adjacent to ocean cells. Since then, the adoption of transient methods of forcing and the development of fully coupled atmosphere–ocean GCMs have brought considerable improvements in the climate model results. Although the significant progress made in modeling future climate, uncertainties still exist.
- Second generation of GCMs: are not fully consistent with each other at the regional scale, and these differences could call their reliability into question. Moreover, reliable results are not yet available at the spatial and temporal resolutions required for many impact studies. One reason for this is that GCMs were not primarily designed for climate-change impact studies, and therefore are not well suited for answering hydrologists' requirements. A second reason is due to the high complexity of the atmospheric processes modelled by GCMs. Refining the spatial resolution would incur extremely heavy computational costs. However, GCMs are the only available tools for the detailed modeling of the future climate, and a key challenge to hydrologists is thus to express the GCM results at a scale more relevant to hydrological studies, to downscale GCM experiment outputs.

2.3. Climate Change Scenarios

Global climate models are widely used to project future climate under the SRES (Special Report on Emissions Scenarios). The future emission scenarios of IPCC (Intergovernmental Panel on Climate Change), were developed on the basis of the social-economic projections (population, technology ...). Thus, four principal scenarios families (A1, A2, B1, and B2) are defined (Table 1).

Table 1. Principal characteristics of (A1, A2, B1, and B2) scenarios families

Scenarios	A1	A2	B1	B2
Population growth	Global population that peaks in mid-century and declines thereafter	Continuously increasing population	Global population that peaks in mid-century and declines thereafter	More increasing than A2
Economic growth	Very rapid	slower and regionally oriented	rapid	moderate
Technological evolution	Introduction of new and more efficient technologies	The worse IPCC future emission scenarios, fragmented technological changes	Rapid with introduction of own technologies	Moderate, local or regional solutions

(Tolika and al., 2012)

The A2 is characterized as pessimistic scenarios in which the CO_2 concentration will increase up to 815 ppm until the end of the century and on global scale temperature will rise from 2.5°C to 4.5°C. In contrast, the B2 scenario, a more optimistic one, is more environmentally base with a smaller mean planetary temperature rise ranging from 1.5°C to 3.0°C (Tolika and al., 2012).

According to Bauwens and al., (2012), to analyze the evolution of climate change, the experts of GIEC defined four paths for emission and concentration of greenhouse gases (GHG's) "the representative concentration pathways (RCPs)". RCPs are time and space dependent trajectories of concentrations of GHG's and pollutants resulting from human activities, including changes in land use. In order to take into account the effects of emissions of all GHGs and aerosols, the RCPs have been chosen based primarily on their emissions, associated concentration outcomes, and net radiative forcing (Table 2) (IPCC, 2007). Then, RCPs provide a quantitative description of concentrations of the climate change pollutants in the atmosphere over time, as well as their radiative forcing in 2100.

Table 2. Types of Representative Concentration Pathways

Name	Radiative Forcing	Concentration	Pathway shapes
RCP 8.5	> 8.5 W/m^2 in 2100	> ~1370 CO_2-eq in 2100	Rising
RCP 6	~ 6 W/m^2 at stabilization After 2100	~850 CO_2-eq (at stabilization after 2100)	Stabilization with overshoot
RCP 4.5	~ 4.5 W/m^2 at stabilization After 2100	~650 CO_2-eq (at stabilization after 2100)	Stabilization with overshoot
RCP 2.6	Peak at ~ 3 W/m^2 before 2100 and then decline	peak at ~490 CO_2-eq before 2100 and then decline	Peak and decline

(IPCC, 2007)

2.3.1. Downscaling Methods

Generally, GCMs run at the global scale with a coarse resolution of 150-300 km. However, it becomes evident that the use of just general circulation models for the analysis of the future changes in the climate characteristics of a complex area could not be considered adequate enough due to their coarse resolution. Assessment of climate change impacts at regional scales usually requires future climate projections at a much finer resolution (in the order of 10 km) (Wang and al., 2014). Over recent years, many downscaling methodologies have been described and tested with the purpose of bridging the gap in the spatial resolution between GCMs and impact models (for hydrology and agriculture). Then, many researchers demonstrate that the development of downscaling methodologies could give a more thorough insight of the expected future changes in the Mediterranean area (Tolika and al., 2012). They can be classified into two main families: Statistical Downscaling (SD) and Dynamical Downscaling (DD).

2.3.1.1. Statistical Downscaling (SD)

Statistical downscaling is based on the view that regional climate is conditioned by two factors: the large scale climatic state which is well resolved by the models, and regional or local physiographic features (topography, land-sea distribution and land use sea) contrast that are not adequately described in the models (Wilby and al., 2004). Indeed, SD includes multiple-regression methods (artificial neural networks (ANN) techniques, and empirical orthogonal function (EOF) analysis, such as the analogue method (Prudhomme and al., 2002). The SD method is suitable for the downscaling of several spatially distributed variables at the daily time step (Boé and al., 2007). Furthermore, Prudhomme and al. (2002), reveals that robust estimates are strongly dependent on the quality and the length of the data series used for the calibration and on the performance of the regression models in capturing the variability of the observed data. Following this approach, an empirical relationship between large-scale information (or predictor(s)) and local variables (or predict ands) is first established for current climate and then applied to derive the regional climate scenario from the large-scale circulation (LSC) simulated by a low resolution model. Originally, the statistical downscaling method used two variables as predictors: the 500 hPa geopotential height (Z500) and the air surface temperature (Boé and al., 2007). This approach is easier to implement with much lower computation requirements (Wilby and al., 2004). A large number of previous research practices have employed statistical techniques to assess climate change impacts at either point or catchment scales. However, statistical downscaling is subject to an unverifiable supposition that the statistical relationships developed for present day climate should hold under different future climate forcing conditions (Wang and al., 2014).

2.3.1.2. Dynamical Downscaling

Dynamical downscaling (DD) is a nested regional climate modeling technique which usually consists of using initial conditions, time-dependent lateral meteorological conditions and surface boundary conditions derived from GCMs or reanalysis of observations to drive high resolution regional climate models (Wang and al., 2014). However, regional-scale limited-area models (LAMs) use GCM outputs as the boundary conditions to calculate estimates at a detailed scale (Prudhomme and al., 2002). The major challenge to the dynamical technique is that regional climate models (RCMs) simulations can be computationally expensive in practice, depending on the domain size, spatial resolution, as well as the simulation length (Wang and al. 2014). Moreover, LAMs are dependent upon the veracity of the GCM grid-point data that are used to drive the boundary conditions of the region (Prudhomme and al., 2002). Dynamical downscaling through the use of higher resolution regional climate models (typically 25-50 km) may still not provide the resolution required for robust hydrological modeling (Majone and al., 2012). Compared with statistical downscaling, the spatial patterns produced are more homogeneous, but not necessarily more realistic. Time-slice, experiments are also considered as dynamical models. These are similar to GCMs, but run only regionally and at a much smaller space-scale (0.5°×0.5°)

and their outputs may be combined with a statistical downscaling approach. They are also computationally expensive and may not simulate precipitation well (Prudhomme and al., 2002).

3. Evapotranspiration: Concept and Determination

3.1. Concept of Evapotranspiration

Evapotranspiration is the combination of soil evaporation and crop transpiration. However, evaporation and transpiration occur simultaneously and there is no easy way of distinguishing between the two processes (Allen and al., 1998). It is used to describe the loss of water from the earth's surface to the atmosphere by the combined process of evaporation from the open water bodies, bare soil and plant surfaces, etc. and transpiration from vegetation or any other moisture living surface (Sadick et al., 2014). Evapotranspiration is the only term that appears in both a water balance equation and a land surface energy balance equation. Estimation of evapotranspiration is essential in a wide range of problems in hydrology, agronomy, forestry and land management, and water resources planning, such as water balance computation, irrigation management, river flow forecasting, ecosystem modeling, etc. (Xu and Singh, 2005).

3.2. Estimation of Evapotranspiration

Several models for estimating evapotranspiration have been introduced in the literature. According to Tegos and al., (2015), the Variety of models is related to the complexity of natural phenomenon and depends on the wide range of input climate data and local climate conditions. According to Adeboye and al., (2009), there are different models for computing reference evapotranspiration and these models are generally classified according to the weather parameters that play the dominant role in the model. These classifications include the temperature-based models such as Thornthwaite (1948); Blaney-Criddle (1950); Hargreaves and Samani (1982). The mass-transfer models which is based on vapor pressure or relative humidity include:

Rohwer (1931) and Harbeck (1962); the radiation models which is based on solar radiation, such as Priestly-Taylor (1972) and Makkink (1957), and the combination models which is based on the energy balance and mass transfer principles and include the Penman (1948), modified Penman and FAO-56 PM (Allen et al., 1998). The availability of many equations for determining evaporation, the wide range of data types needed (Allen and al., 1998), and the wide range of expertise needed to use the various equations correctly make it difficult to select the most appropriate evaporation method for a given study (Xu and Singh, 2002).

3.2.1. Empirical and Semi Empirical Evapotranspiration Models

Due the lack of experimental measurements and the increasing availability of more and more reliable standard climatic data through improving networks of meteorological stations have led to the development of a wide variety of estimation models (empirical and semi-empirical) in the last decades. The choice of a model usually depends on the specific climatic inputs that are available in the test station and on the previous performance of a model in a similar climatic context (Marti and al., 2015). We find mainly two categories of formulae (Temperature and radiation formula).

3.2.1.1. Temperatures Based ET Models

The temperature based ET models were developed to estimate evapotranspiration on a low temporal resolution (for example months). However one can test how they perform on a daily or even hourly resolution, too.

Blaney and Criddle (1950)

Based on temperature and the yearly sum of astronomic possible sunshine duration, Blaney and Criddle derived the following formula to estimate potential evapotranspiration

$$ETP = k * (0{,}46 * T + 8{,}13) * P(Dj)$$

With:
ETP: reference evapotranspiration (mm/month)
T: monthly air temperature (°C)
K: cultural coefficient,
P(Dj): corrective term bound on daytime hours Dj

The application of various models to estimate annual evapotranspiration in the region of Djelfa (semi-arid zone), shows that Blany and Criddle models seems to provide good estimation of this climatic component. However, during the period 1996-2001, this approach underestimate evapotranspiration (Bouteldjaoui and al., 2011). According to Viau and al., (1992), in Trinidad and Tobago (Tropical countries), the Blaney-Criddle approach seems to provide better results based on the fact that daily errors are of the order of 10% while the error over one month is about 2%.

Hargreaves (Hargreaves and Samani, 1985)

The model to estimate evapotranspiration after Hargreaves is a strongly empirical model. Both, radiation and temperature are used as input data. Advantageous is, that no radiation has to be measured. However, where solar radiation, wind speed, relative humidity and other data are completely absent, reference evapotranspiration can also be estimated using the equation stated by Hargreaves and Samani (1985) (Adeboye, 2009).

$$ETP = 0{,}0023 R_a * (T_{mean} + 17{,}8) * \sqrt{(T_{\max} - T_{\min})}$$

where:

ETo: daily reference evapotranspiration (mm/day)
Tmax, Tmin: maximum and minimum daily temperatures (°C)
Tmean: mean temperature (°C)
Ra: the extraterrestrial radiation Mj m^{-2} day^{-1}

Hargreaves equation was the best model to estimate evapotranspiration in eastern arid and semiarid regions of Iran, bat it was shown to overestimate evapotranspiration under the humid conditions of northeast Louisiana's climate (Djaman and al., 2015). According to Jabloun and Sahli (2008), results obtained from the comparison of evapotranspiration daily estimates by the Hargreaves model against FAO-56 PM, throughout eight stations in the semi-arid Tunisia, showed that in inland stations, Hargreaves tends to overestimate ETo due to high ΔT values. In the coastal station of Tunisia, Hargreaves underestimated ETo values, which they attributed to an underestimation of Rs. Thus, further research is required to adjust the Hargreaves coefficients to local conditions for obtaining a better accuracy. Moreover, the comparison of three evapotranspiration model (Hargreaes, PM FAO-56 and Jensen haise) in three region from Nigeria, showed that, when complete data were used in the computation, Hargreaves model overestimated evapotranspiration However, under limited data set, Hargreaves model underestimated evapotranspiration (Adeboye, 2009).

3.2.1.2. Radiation Based ET Model Turc (1961)

The method after Turc was developed for France and North Africa. As in the Hargreaves equation, not only radiation, but also temperature is used as input parameters. The Formula after Turc is only defined for temperatures above zero, and gets inaccurate at low temperatures.

For RH ≥ 50%:

$$ETP = 0{,}4(R_G + 50)(T/(T+15))$$

(For February, substitute 0,40 with 0,37)

For HR<50%

$$ETP(mm/month) = 0{,}4(R_G + 50)(T/(T+15))(1+((50-RH)/70))$$

(For February, substitute 0,40 with 0,37)

where:

PET: Evapotranspiration after Turc mm/month
R_G : Global radiation cal/cm^2/month
T: Average air temperature/month (°C)

The reliability of Turc method strongly depends on wind speed, with overestimation under low wind speeds and underestimation during windy periods (Minacapilli and al., 2015). Djaman and al., (2015), reported that the evaluation of sixteen reference evapotranspiration equations against ASCE-PM model under the Sahelian condition at Ndiaye and Fanaye (Sebegal), showed that Turc equation systematically underestimate ET_0. In contrast, numerous studies noted that the Turc radiation-based method showed promise with in the southeastern United States under data limited conditions. Moreover, Turc method was the best suited model in cold humid and arid climate. Then, in the absence of regionally-calibrated Turc equation is recommended for estimating reference evapotranspiration using measured maximum and minimum air temperature and estimated radiation in Florida (Djaman and al., 2015).

Priestley –Taylor (1972)

The Priestley-Taylor equation to estimate evapotranspiration is a simplification of the FAO Penman-Monteith equation, where the aerodynamic part is neglected. It only needs net radiation and temperature to calculate ETP. This simplification is based on the fact that ETP is more dependent on radiation than on relative humidity and wind.

$$ETP = \alpha * \Delta/(\Delta + \gamma) * (R_n / \lambda)$$

where:

ETP: reference evapotranspiration (mm/day)
Δ: Slope of vapor pressure curve ($KPa°C^{-1}$)
γ: Psychometric constant ($KPa.°C^{-1}$)
Rn: Net radiation at the crop surface ($Mj.m^{-2}.j^{-1}$)
α: Priestley-Taylor parameter (1,26);
λ: latent heat of vaporization ($Mj.m^{-2}\ mm^{-1}$)

In sicily, Priestley-Taylor model was calibrated with Scintillometer data to determine the best parameter (value of the constant) for the study area. Better performance of Priestley-Taylor model can be obtained when a value of α =1.09 is considered in place of the original α=1.26 proposed by the Authors (Carmelo and al., 2012). Moreover, in Switzerland, the comparison of five evapotranspiration models against Penman-Monteith method, showed that Prestley-Taylor model is the most suitable under such climatic environment (Xu and Singh., 2002).

3.2.1.3. Physically-Based Etmodels Penman-Monteith

A large number of empirical methods have been developed over the last 50 years to estimate evapotranspiration from different climatic variables. Some of these derived from the now well-known Penman equation (Penman, 1948) to determine evaporation from open water, bare soil and grass (now called evapotranspiration) based on a combination of an energy balance and an aerodynamic formula. Various derivation of the Penman equation included a bulk surface resistance term (Monteith, 1965) and the resulting equation is now called the Penman-Monteith equation, which may be expressed for daily values as:

$$ETP = (\Delta * R_n + (\rho * c_p(e_a - e)/r_a)/(\lambda\rho_w(\Delta + \gamma(1 + r_s/r_a)))$$

ρ: air density (kg/m^3),
cp :specific heat of dry air ($J\ kg^{-1}C^{-1}$),
ρw : masse volumique de l'eau (ρw = 1000 kg/m^3),
ra : bulk surface aerodynamic resistance for water vapor ($s\ m^{-1}$)
rs : canopy surface resistance ($s\ m^{-1}$).
Δ : Slope of vapor pressure curve (Pa $°C^{-1}$),
Rn : Net radiation ($J/m^2/j$),
γ: Psychometric constant (Pa $°C^{-1}$)
ea: mean saturated vapor pressure (Pa)
e: mean daily ambient vapor pressure (Pa).

FAO-Penman Monteith

The Penman-Monteith formulation was proposed by FAO as the standard method for computing Potential or Reference Evapotranspiration (ETo). It has been recommended as the best for the reference evapotranspiration (ETo) estimates. The FAO Penman-Monteith method (FAO-PM) has had numerous successful applications in hydrology and agrometeorology in various hydroclimatic regimes (Malamos and al., 2015).

$$ETP = (0{,}408\Delta R_n + \gamma(900/(T + 237))u_2(e_a - e))/(\Delta + \gamma(1 + 0{,}34u_2))$$

where: ETo: Reference evapotranspiration (mm day^{-1}),
Rn: net radiation at the crop surface ($MJm^{-2}\ day^{-1}$),
G: soil heat flux density ($MJm^{-2}\ day^{-1}$),
T: mean daily air temperature at 2 m height (°C),
u_2: wind speed at 2 m height ($m\ s^{-1}$),
e_a: saturation vapour pressure (kPa),
e: actual vapour pressure (kPa),
e_a _ e : the saturation vapour pressure deficit (kPa),
Δ: slope of the vapour pressure curve (kPa $°C^{-1}$)
γ: psychrometric constant (kPa $°C^{-1}$).

The FAO-56 Penman–Monteith method is the most adequate for calculating average daily ETo. The use of this improved method is limited due to the availability and quality of the required data (Jabloun and Sahli, 2008). According to Minicapilli and al., (2015), different methods to estimate ET_0

were tested in a typical Mediterranean environment (Sicily) by means of comparisons against scintillometric measurements carried out on alfalfa reference crop during spring-summer of 2005. The results confirm that FAO-56 formulation represents the best approach to estimate ET_0 at both hourly and daily time. However, it is characterized by the lowest mean bias error (-0.15 mm d^{-1} and 0.06 mm d^{-1}) using daily or hourly data, respectively.

4. Climate Change Effects on Evapotranspiration

In modern societies, potential water resource conflicts arise as a consequence of current multiple uses (industrial, agriculture, ecosystems, and human consumption) as well as increasing demand due to population growth (Silva and al., 2010). Global climate changes and intensified human activities have induced significant impacts on ecological environments, such as the high frequency of drought disasters and drying up in many river basins. Therefore, it is necessary to wonder about the consequences of this warming on the water cycle in general and in the Mediterranean region in particular. Indeed, this region is probably more susceptible to climate change as, geographically, it lies in a transition area between the hot, dry climate of Africa and the cold, humid air masses arriving from northern Europe. The consequences of these possible changes in climate are all the more worrying in the Mediterranean region as socioeconomic scenarios indicate an increase in population and hence growing human pressure on water resources (Chaouche and al., 2010). In Mediterranean regions, the situation could become more critical since current imbalances between water supply and demand which are aggravated as a consequence of climate change. Several models predict that precipitation is likely to be reduced in the next decades affecting runoff processes. In addition, temperature increases will produce changes in seasonality of stream flow associated with early snowmelt (Silva and al., 2010). Moreover, climate model ensembles predict future decreases in precipitation over southern Europe indicating that annual precipitation is very likely to decrease in the Mediterranean area while the risk of summer drought is likely to increase (Majone and al., 2012).

Changes in climatic factors also affected all elements of hydrologic cycle, such as precipitation, evapotranspiration, runoff, and groundwater flow in a variety of ways (Zhang and al., 2015). According to Prudhomme and al (2002), many climate change impact studies have, in the past, focused on assessing the potential implication of global warming in terms of water resources at a national or regional level. Additionally to the effects on runoff through the changes of temperature and precipitation, climate change influences evaporation to a high degree (Zhang and al., 2015). In the context of climate change, changes of temperature, wind speed, rainfall, solar radiation and other factors will lead to the change of evapotranspiration, thus affecting the plan of crop water demand and agricultural water usage.

Syndro and al., (2011), showed that, in addition to rising temperatures, increasing humidity and higher CO_2 concentrations can also affect evapotranspiration. However, they often tend to reduce transpiration and counteract the higher temperature effects on ETo. As the oceans and other water bodies warm and evaporate more water into the atmosphere, global humidity is likely to increase. When CO_2 concentrations increase, leaf stomata partially close to maintain the CO_2 concentration inside the stomata. Thus, while climate change is likely to increase air temperature, the effect of higher humidity and CO_2 concentration could partially offset the temperature effect on evapotranspiration. Standardized Penman-Monteith equation for short canopy reference evapotranspiration (ETo) and scenarios for possible changes in temperature, humidity, and CO_2, reported on the likely impact of these changes on ETo. It was assumed that aerodynamic resistance will remain unchanged and the grass does not experience water stress. If the canopy resistance increases in response to higher CO_2 and the dew point temperature increases, the results indicate that little or no change in ETo is likely due to increasing air temperature. The impact of global warming on ETo will probably be less in locations with higher wind speeds.

In the same context, Khalil (2013), studied the effect of climate change on evapotranspiration in Egypt. However, the results from general circulation model of HadCM3 data for four scenarios A1, A2, B1 and B2 reveals that mean temperature has increased and the maximum increase will happen in 2100. The comparison between evapotranspiration during the years (2000-2009) and future climate during the years (2040, 2060, 2080 and 2100) at 20 studied weather stations revealed a general increase in evapotranspiration under future climate for scenarios (A1, A2, and B1and B2). Then, water consumption under climate change in Egypt should be developed to reduce the negative effects of climate change on evapotranspiration. However, the evapotranspiration increased under climate change in comparison with control one. A2 scenario at 2100 gave the highest ETo and B1 scenario at 2040 gave the lowest ETo in comparison with other scenarios. This study reveals that water requirements will be increased under climate change conditions due to increase ETo (Khalil, 2013).

On the western part of the French Mediterranean area, water resources (surface and groundwater) are sensitive to climate change. The study addresses the question of whether any trend in the annual and monthly series of temperature, rainfall and potential evapotranspiration already appears at the scale of this region. The trends observed in 13 catchments of interest are consistent with those observed at a larger scale. The results showed an increase in annual mean temperature and annual evapotranspiration was observed throughout the study area, whereas annual precipitation has not exhibited any trend. The monthly scale has revealed strong seasonal variability in trend. The trend for an increase in monthly evapotranspiration has been observed mainly in the spring, and has not been seen in the coastal areas. A trend for an increase in monthly temperature has been observed in June and in the spring throughout the entire area. Monthly rainfall has been found to decrease in June and increase in November throughout the area (Chaouche and al., 2010).

CONCLUSION

In many arid and semi-arid countries, especially in the Mediterranean regions, water is being more and more scarce. Mediterranean countries are declared to be the most vulnerable region in the world to climate change. In addition to several weather conditions such as increased floods, global climate change causes lower and more erratic rainfall combined with increased temperature, then resulting in higher evaporation and water demand. Changes in climatic factors also can affected all elements of hydrologic cycle, such as precipitation, evapotranspiration, runoff, and groundwater flow in a variety of ways. However, the approach to estimate climate change impacts on water resources consist on union between climate model outputs and hydrological models. In this context, recent developments in climate change project using global and regional climate models made it possible to provide more detailed information on temperature and precipitation changes. Different studies reveals that in Mediterranean regions, the impact of global warming will lead to the change of evapotranspiration, thus affecting the plan of crop water demand and agricultural water usage. In the one Hand, water requirements will be increased under climate change conditions due to increase ETo. Therefore, the impact of global warming on ETo will probably be less in locations with higher wind speeds. In the other hand, climate change is likely to increase air temperature, the effect of higher humidity and CO_2 concentration could partially offset the temperature effect on evapotranspiration.

REFERENCES

Adeboye, O.B., Osunbitan, J.A., Adekalu1, K.O. and Okunade, D.A. (2009). Evaluation of FAO-56 Penman Monteith and Temperature Based Models in Estimating Reference Evapotranspiration: *Agricultural Engineering International,* 11.

Allen, RG., Pereira, L.S., Raes, D. and Smith, M. (1998). Crop evapotranspiration-Guidelines for computing crop water requirements-*FAO Irrigation and drainage paper* 56, Rome: FAO.

Bauwens. A., Sohier. C. and Degré A. (2012). Impacts du changement climatique sur l'hydrologie et la gestion des ressources en eau du bassin de la Meuse: *Biotechnol. Agron. Soc. Environ*, 76-86.

Boé, J., Terray, L., Habet, B. and Martin, E. (2007). Statistical and dynamical downscaling of the Seine basin climate for hydro-meteorological studies: *International Journal of Climatology*, 27, 1643-1655.

Bouteldjaoui, F., Bessenasse, M. and Guendouz A. (2011). Etude comparative des différentes méthodes d'estimation de l'évapotranspiration en zone semi-aride (cas de la région de Djelfa): *Nature and Technologie,* 8, 109-116.

Carmelo, A., Carmelo, C., Mario, M., Giuseppe, P. and Giovanni, R. (2012). Testing approach to estimate hourly reference evapotranspiration with scintillometer measurements under mediterranean climate: conference paper, Italie.

Minacapilli, M., Cammalleri, C., Ciraolo, G., Giovanni, R. and Giuseppe, P. (2015). Using scintillometry to assess reference evapotranspiration methods and their impact on the water balance of olive groves: *Agricultural Water Management,* 1-12.

Chaouche, K., Neppel, K., Dieulin, C., Pujol, N., Ladouche, B., Martin, E., Salas. and Caballero, Y. (2010). Analyses of precipitation, temperature and evapotranspiration in a French Mediterranean region in the context of climate change: *Comptes Rendus Geoscience*, 10, 234-243.

Dastorani, M.T. and Poormohammadi, S. (2012). Evaluation of the Effects of Climate Change on Temperature, Precipitation and Evapotranspiration in Iran: *International Conference on Applied Life Sciences*, 73-79.

Djaman, K., Balde, A.B., Sow, A., Muller, B., Irmak, S., N'Diaye, M., Manneh, B., Moukoumbi, Y.D., Futakuchi, K. and Saito, K. (2015). Evaluation of sixteen reference evapotranspiration methods under Sahelian conditions in the Senegal River Valley: *Journal of hydrology: Regional studies,* 20, 139-159.

IPCC. (2007). Summary for Policymakers. In: Climate Change 2007: Impacts, Adaptation and Vulnerability, Contribution of Working Group II to the Fourth Assessment Report of the Intergovernmental Panel on Climate Change, Parry, M.L., Canziani, O.F., Palutikof, J.P., van der Linden, P.J. and Hanson, C.E, Cambridge University Press, 7-22.

IPCC. (2008). Technical Summary. Towards New Scenarios for Analysis of Emissions, Climate Change, Impacts, and Response Strategies. Intergovernmental Panel on Climate Change. Moss,R., Babiker, M., Brinkman,S., Calvo, E., Carter, T., Edmonds, J., Elgizouli, I., Emori, S., Erda, L., Hibbard, K., Jones, R., Kainuma, M., Kelleher, J., Lamarque, J.F., Manning, M., Matthews, B., Meehl, J., Meyer, L., Mitchell, L., Nakicenovic, N., O'Neill, B., Pichs, R., Riahi, K., Rose, S., Runci, P., Stouffer, R., van Vuuren, D., Weyant, J., Wilbanks, T., van Ypersele, J.P. and Zurek, M. 25.

Jabloun, M. and Sahli, A. (2008). Evaluation of FAO-56 methodology for estimating reference evapotranspiration using limited climatic data Application to Tunisia: *Agricaltural water management*, 10, 707-715.

Khalil, A.A. (2013). *Effect of climate change on evapotranspiration in Egypt*, 5, 7-12.

Le Treut, H. (2003). Les scénarios globaux de changement climatique et leurs incertitudes: *Comptes Rendus Géoscience*, 525- 533.

Majone, B., Bovolo, C. I., Bellin, A., Blenkinsop, S. and Fowler, H. J. (2012), Modeling the impacts of future climate change on water resources for the Gallego river basin (Spain): *Water Resources Research*, 48, 1-18.

Martía, P., González-Altozanob, P., López-Urreac, R., Manchad, L.A. and Shiri, J. (2015). Modeling reference evapotranspiration with calculated targets. Assessment and implications: *Agricultural Water Management*, 10, 81-90.

Malamos, N., Barouchas, P.E., Tsirogiannis, I.L., Liopa-Tsakalidi, A. and Koromilas,Th. (2015). Estimation of monthly FAO Penman-Monteith evapotranspiration in GIS environment, through a geometry independent algorithm: Agriculture and Agricultural Science Procedia, 10, 209-299.

Murphy, J. (1998). An Evaluation of statistical and dynamical techniques for downscaling local climate: *Journal of Climate*, 12, 2256- 2283.

Prudhomme, Ch., Reynard, N. and Crooks, S. (2002). Downscaling of global climate models for flood frequency analysis: where are we now?: *Hydrological processes*, 16, 1137-1150.

Ravazzani, G., Ghilard,i M., Mendlik, T., Gobiet, A., Corbari, C. and Mancini, M. (2014). Investigation of Climate Change Impact on Water Resources for an Alpine Basin in Northern Italy: Implications for Evapotranspiration Modeling Complexity: *PLOS ONE*, 9, 1-10.

Sadick, A., Ansah., I.O., Badu, A.O., Nketia, K.A., Asamoah, E., Asaana, J. and Amfo-Out, R. (2014). Estimation of Potential Evapotranspiration at Botanga Irrigation Scheme in the Northern Region of Ghana: *Environmental Research, Engineering and Management*, 8, 5-13.

Silva, D., Meza, F.J. and Varas, E. (2010). Estimating reference evapotranspiration (ETo) using numerical weather forecast data in central Chile: *Journal of Hydrology*, 8, 64-71.

Snyder, R. L., Moratiel, R., Song, Z. W., Swelam, A., Jomaa, I. and Shapland, T. (2011). Evapotranspiration Response to Climate Change: *Acta Hortic,* 922, 91-98.

Tegos, A., Efstratiais, A., Malamos, N., Mamassis, N. and Koutsoyiannis, D. (2015). Evaluation of a parametric appraoch for estimating potentiel evapotranspiration across different climates: *Agriculture and agricultural science procedia*, 8, 2-9.

Timbal, B., Fernandez, E., Li, Z. (2008). Generalization of a statistical downscaling model to provide local climate change projections for Australia: *Environmental Modelling and Software*, 24, 341-358.

Tolika, C.K., Zanis, P. and Anagnostopoulou, C. (2012). Regional climate change scenarios for greece: future temperature and precipitation projections from ensembles of RCMs: Global NEST Journal, 14, 407-421.

Viau, A., Boivin, J. and Singh, B. (1992). Étude comparative d'approches utilisées pour l'estimation de l'évapotranspiration en régions tropicales: *Climatological Bulletin*, 19,106-124.

Wang, X., Huang, G., Lin, Q., Niea, X. and Liud, J. (2014). High-resolution temperature and precipitation projections over Ontario, Canada: a coupled dynamical-statistical approach: *Journal of the Royal Meteorological Society,* 1-10.

Wilby, R.L., Charles, S.P., Zorita, E., Timbal, B., Whetton, P. and Mearns, L.O., 2004. *Guidlines for use of climate scenarios developed from statistical downscaling methods*, 27.

Xu, C.Y. and Singh, V.P. (2002). Cross Comparison of Empirical Equations for Calculating Potential Evapotranspiration with Data from Switzerland: *Water Resources Management*, 23,197-219.

Xu, C.Y. and Singh, V.P. (2005). Evaluation of three complementary relationship evapotranspiration models by water balance approach to estimate actual regional evapotranspiration in different climatic regions: *Journal of Hydrology*, 16, 105-121.

Zhang, K.X., Pan, S. m., Zhang, W., Xu, Y. h., Cao, L. g., Hao, Y. p., Wang, Y. (2015). Influence of climate change on reference evapotranspiration and aridity index and their temporal spatial variations in the Yellow River Basin, China, from 1961 to 2012: *Quaternary International*, 75-82.

INDEX

A

B

C

D

Q

R

S

T

U

V

W

Y